Editorial

FIONA SAMPSON

*P*sycho-geographies: hardly an original term. But what else to call the complex set of dialectics, not one but many, by which a personality and the place it inhabits shape each other? We're formed by culture, historical moment, and the physical setting in which we find ourselves: just as we in turn contribute to social and family culture, and work upon our environment – hang laundry on balconies, graze cattle on boggy pasture which they poach, work in construction. Poets, pace the Wordsworth of *Lyrical Ballads*, aren't exceptional, but unexceptional, in the way their psyches reflect and contribute to the world around them.

All the same, some poets seem particularly aware of what we might give in and call that Marxian dialectic. In this issue of *Poetry Review*, John Kinsella completes a series of essays about reading and writing the Australian landscape. Kinsella's poetry forms part of his wider environmental activism. On the other hand, when Paul Farley uses Louis MacNeice's landscapes to read the poet, he traces their conversion to symbol within MacNeice's work – and uses those symbols to guide his own readings. Tom Lowenstein is a poet of the radical 60s generation. Here we publish an extract from his account of life with an Inuit community. If Lowenstein's engagement with this particular life-world is voluntary and responsible, no less responsible, albeit involuntary, is Oksana Zabuzhko's account of how recent Ukrainian history is inseparable from her writing life.

This issue of *PR* includes major poems mapping psyche and place by C.K. Williams, Hugo Williams, Martin Harrison and – translated by Elaine Feinstein – Marina Tsvetaeva. But *Psycho-geographies* also celebrates another poet of dis/location. Peter Porter, poetry's most famous Australian-in-exile, celebrated his eightieth birthday (in February) with the publication of a major new collection. *Better Than God* is a vigorous, moving – and terrifying – continuation of his life-long engagement with the truth and limit of the European take on what it means to be human. Porter's commitment to poetry in Britain has generated – and indeed shaped – an extraordinary cohort of admirers both here and there, from among the finest poets of their respective generations. We publish some of their homages; and, later in the magazine, Porter himself chooses the best work by an unpublished poet from the year's *Review*.

This quarter has been a sad one for British poetry, with the loss within a single month of Harold Pinter, Adrian Mitchell, John Fairfax and Mick Imlah

– and, as we go to press, of Edward Upward. Imlah, who edited *Poetry Review* from 1984-86, was a poet, editor and critic of real seriousness (and not a little intellectual mischievousness). His last book, the twenty years'-worth of poems which comprise *The Lost Leader*, explores Scottishness from many angles; yet as Editor at the *Review* he explored things as English as Larkin, as metropolitan as literary gossip, and as British as Geoffrey Hill, with fluent intelligence. That relatively rare thing, a poet-editor, he makes an exemplary role model for an era in which it would be all too easy to value reputation over the actual reading of poetry.

ℬ

Dorothy Sargent Rosenberg Annual Poetry Prizes, 2009

Prizes ranging from $1,000 up to as much as $25,000 will be awarded for the finest lyric poems celebrating the human spirit. The contest is open to all writers, published or unpublished, who will be under the age of 40 on November 6, 2009. Entries must be postmarked on or before the third Saturday in October (October 17, 2009). Only previously unpublished poems are eligible for prizes. Names of prize winners will be published on our website on February 5, 2010, together with a selection of the winning poems. Please visit our website www.DorothyPrizes.org for further information and to read poems by previous winners.

Checklist of Contest Guidelines
- Entries must be postmarked on or before October 17, 2009.
- Past winners may re-enter until their prizes total in excess of $25,000.
- All entrants must be under the age of 40 on November 6, 2009.
- Submissions must be original, previously unpublished, and in English: no translations, please.
- Each entrant may submit one to three separate poems.
- Only one of the poems may be more than thirty lines in length.
- Each poem must be printed on a separate sheet.
- Submit two copies of each entry with your name, address, phone number and email address clearly marked on each page of one copy only.
- Include an index card with your name, address, phone number and email address and the titles of each of your submitted poems.
- Include a $10 entry fee payable to the Dorothy Sargent Rosenberg Memorial Fund. (This fee is not required for entries mailed from outside the U.S.A.)
- Poems will not be returned. Inc. a stamped addressed envelope if you wish us to acknowledge receipt of your entry.

MAIL ENTRIES TO: Dorothy Sargent Rosenberg Poetry Prizes, PO Box 2306, Orinda, California 94563, USA

Contents

Volume 99:1 Spring 2009

Centrefold

Reviews And Endpapers

POEMS

...sparkling in their chances...
— *Peter Porter*

C.K. Williams
Either / Or

1.

My dream after the dream of more war: that for every brain
there exists a devil, a particular devil, hairy, scaly or slimy,
but compact enough to slot between lobes, and evil, implacably evil,
slicing at us from within, causing us to yield to the part
of the soul that argues itself to pieces, then reconstitutes as a club.

When I looked closely, though, at my world, it seemed to me devils
were insufficient to account for such terror, confusion, and hatred:
evil must be other than one by one, one at a time, it has to be general,
a palpable something like carbon-dioxide or ash that bleeds
over the hemispheres of the world as over the halves of the mind.

But could it really be that overarching? What of love, generosity,
pity? So I concluded there after all would have to be devils,
but mine, when I dug through the furrows to find him, seemed listless,
mostly he spent his time honing his horns – little pronged things
like babies' erections, but sharp, sharp as the blade that guts the goat.

2.

Just as in the brain are devils, in the world are bees: bees are angels,
angels bees. Each person has his or her bee, and his or her angel,
not "guardian angel," not either one of those with "…drawn swords…"
who "…inflict chastisement…" but angels of presence, the presence
that flares in the conscience not as philosophers' fire, but bees'.

Bee-fire is love, angel-fire is too: both angels and bees evolve
from seen to unseen; both as you know from your childhood
have glittering wings but regarded too closely are dragons. Both,
like trappers, have fur on their legs, sticky with lickings of pollen:
for angels the sweetness is maddening; for bees it's part of the job.

Still, not in their wildest imaginings did the angel-bees reckon
to labor like mules, be trucked from meadow to mountain,
have their compasses fouled so they'd fall on their backs,
like old men, like me, dust to their diamond, dross to their ore,
but wondering as they do who in this cruel strew of matter will save us.

Peter Porter
A Chorale At The Crossing

Ihr Gatten, die ihr liebend euch in Armen liegt,
ihr sind die Brücke, überm Abgrund ausgespannt,
auf der die Toten wiederum ins Leben gehn!
Geheiligt sei eurer Liebe Werk!
– Hugo von Hofmannsthal

But that one who is the every always one
May still be a surprise – if she's whom
That time you betrayed and this time rebuked,
Who, while you were thinking of another
Startled you by not wanting to be with you
Though you'd excused all othernesses
By resolving to make her the true centre
Of existence; accepting that this was
Accounting, a way of excusing betrayal
By ordering responsibility –
Then, and no surprise after all
It should be so, the uncontrollable dream
Showed not her but you; not life but death.

This might be the message of the bridge the dead
Walk over: they are sparkling in their chances
However undeserving; they have been dressed
In time's immeasurability;
One life could never be enough; their tunes
Are faces, their words perfectly understandable
Yet have no meaning. This side of the bridge
There is a toll – it's like the seventy stairs
You have been up and down a million times;
It is paid in lifetime familiarity.
Now they are seen to be carrying, everyone
The same burden, the command to love,
Where some object might exist as proof
Or all the stars collate the obligation.

Elaine Feinstein
Lyrics from Marina Tsvetaeva's *Girlfriend*

1.
Are you happy? You never tell me.
        Maybe it's better like this.
You've kissed so many others,
        and that's a sadness.

In you, I see the heroines
        of Shakespeare's tragedies.
You, my tragic lady, were
        never saved by anybody.

You have grown tired of repeating
        the familiar words of love!
An iron ring on a bloodless hand
        is more expressive.

I love you – like a storm burst
        overhead – I confess it;
the more fiercely because you burn
        and bite, and most of all

because our secret lives take such
        very different paths:
seduction and dark fate
        are your inspiration.

To you, my aquiline demon,
        I apologise. In a flash –
as if over a coffin – I realise
        it was always too late to save you!

Even as I tremble – it may be
        I am dreaming – there
remains one enchanting irony:
        for *you* – are not *he.*

6.
Night weeps over coffee grounds
     as it looks to the east.
Its mouth is a tender blossom
     but it has a monstrous flower.

Soon a young, thin moon will take
     the place of scarlet dawn,
and I shall give you many
     combs and rings.

The young moon between the branches
     never guards anyone.
I shall give you bracelets,
     chains and ear-rings!

Your bright eyes sparkle, as if
     from under a heavy mane.
Are your horses jealous – those
     thoroughbreds, so light on their feet?

10.
How can I forget that perfume
     of White Rose and tea,
those figures of Sèvre above
     a blazing fireplace.

There we stood. I was dressed
     in splendid golden silk.
You – in a black knit jacket
     with a winged collar.

As you entered, I remember your face
        was almost colorless;
you stood biting a finger,
        your head slightly tilted.

A helmet of red hair surrounded
        your powerful forehead.
You were neither woman nor boy –
        but stronger than I was.

With no reason to move, I stood up
        and at once people gathered round –
someone even tried, as if in a joke,
        to introduce us.

How calmly you put
        your hand in mine,
and left in my palm a lingering
        splinter of ice.

You took out a cigarette,
        I offered you a light,
afraid of what I might do
        if you looked into my face.

I remember how our glasses clinked
        over a blue vase. *Please
be my Orestes*, I murmured
        – and gave you a flower.

Your grey eyes flashed as you took
        a handkerchief out of your
black suede purse – and slowly
        let it drop to the floor.

13.
Let me repeat, at the end of our love
        on the very eve of parting,
how much I loved those powerful
        hands of yours,

those eyes which do – or don't –
        look someone over, and
nevertheless demand a report
        on my most casual glance.

Three times is your passion cursed!
        God sees all of you
and insists on repentance
        for every casual sigh.

Now let me say again, wearily
        – don't hurry to listen –
your soul now stands
        in the way of my own.

And something else, since
        it is almost evening –
that mouth of yours was young
        when we first kissed,

your gaze was bold and light then
        your being – five years old...
How fortunate are those
        who have not crossed your path.

Hugo Williams
from Poems To My Mother

"You're the top, you're an ocean liner.
You're the top, you're Margaret Vyner."
– Cole Porter

1. The Cull

You sit with your address book
open on your knee,
gently but firmly
crossing out the names
of old friends who have died.
"I wonder what happened
to Kay Morrow?" you ask.
"It doesn't matter,
I never liked her really."
Your pen hovers briefly
over the head of the bridesmaid
we've heard so much about,
then slices her in two.

You have the look of a job well done
as stragglers are rounded up
for demolition.
"Dear old Denny Moon!
He taught me to ride.
He used to jump out from behind a tree
cracking a banksia whip.
That, or driving an old Lancia
between kerosene tins."
You shake your head at him.
In spite of all the fun
you smile with quiet satisfaction
as you let him slip away.

2. New South Wales 1920

A hundred miles ahead of the drought
and behind on the payments
you were on your way
to start a new life in New South Wales
when the car broke down
under a coolabar tree
and your father said it was The End.

He made you get down
and wait in the shade of the tree
while he went and stood on his own.
You thought you had arrived in New South Wales
and could start to explore,
till you looked behind the tree
and saw the bush stretching away.

He brought your luggage over
to where you were sitting
and started sprinkling petrol over the car.
You thought he was cooling it down
and giving it a clean,
before you set out once more
for your new life in New South Wales.

4. Someone's Girlfriend

"I'd met him before of course, at somewhere like
Government House in Sydney, then again
in a nightclub in Le Touquet, doing my nut
trying to get him to light my cigarette.
I'd heard he was going to be in this
Freddie Lonsdale play on Broadway, 'Half a Loaf',
so I got my agent to fix me an interview
with the director, Gilbert Miller,
who threw me the part of someone's girlfriend.
When your father saw me sitting there
in the dining room of the SS Washington,
drinking my glass of milk, he thought he'd just
discovered me. He sent a note to my table
saying 'Champagne better than milk,
why don't you join me?'
                              I remember it was evening
when we arrived in New York Harbour.
Guy Middleton and Frank Lawton came down
to meet the boat in their dinner jackets
and took us back to a party. Your father and I
were staying at The Gotham, but it wasn't long
before we moved to The Devil, which was just as well,
I suppose, considering he was still married."

6. A Conjuring Trick

in memoriam M.V.

The undertaker slips me a folded envelope
in which he has caused to appear
her teeth and wedding ring.
His hand closes over mine.
His smile seems to require my approval
for his conjuring trick.

I feel inclined to applaud his skill
in so reducing flesh and bone
to this brief summary,
until I see his scuffed grey moccasins
and moth-eaten opera hat
with the folding mechanism showing through.

He takes me aside
and whispers that her ashes
will be waiting for me in Reception.
As we crunch back to the cars, we turn
and see smoke spiralling into the air,
while something difficult is imagined.

Michael Murphy
Black And Gray

Against the backdrop of constellations
the light is growing shorter, a mirror
turned like a face to the wall.

And passing beneath them, between
shadows hovering among shadows,
a candle and candle-flame, cupped hands.

*

Loosening your hair, brushing it out
into streams, the light growing longer, it is
like another day, as light as stone.

The moon leading us home by any route
its shadow runs at our feet
like another day, as light as stone.

*

We might be burning autumn in the allotment,
three sparrows scratching a living.
Racing apart among the dying stars

Mars and Venus, Orion and the Pleiades
looking down, break their hearts
among leaf-shadow, between worlds.

*

And water, what I thought was myself
as fire frozen in the bedroom window,
was like nothing else, nothing else again.

Black and Gray: window frames, mirrors
falling through fingers, a sieve, a half-
light passing elsewhere through the door.

Jane Holland
Sapphic: Jamesian, Aureate

The Golden Bowl, you were,
     and I a crack
across that gorgeous patina.

Almost too much to break, to speak,
     disturb the dust
in a backstreet antique shop.

But you were something else
and something else again: a silence
     broken, after rain.

Where are you now? So bright, intense:
     O shining girl,
          my private Her,
the light that hammers every line.

Martin Harrison
[Wallabies]

...some memories from somewhere those scattered trees
that straggle of white tree limbs like bleached bones

perhaps a line from someone else or myself
memory of the flattest waters I've ever seen

emerging dreamlike from the low brown skyline
bouquets of white cockatoos bursting from the leaves

out-of-time movement over the dead stubble
what've they been doing? they've been hiding

they've always been there in the mind, in the body
and then some images of suddenly meeting

that low brown water's thin mirror
as if the crowd of trees signalled to it, or had been

signalling all their lives, building riverine clusters,
building their wandering cicatrice seen from far off –

but when you get there it's the necessary damage
of banks and flooded logs, dried up pools, Toyota paths

nestled spots to fish from the ones safe to swim
flickering shadows hands of them sweeping over the sand

that sense too of clayed ground of earth dust grit pebbles
shards of bark crumbling the crumble and dust of leaves

earth hard with veins of muddy tree roots showing there
wooden dark veins jutting through aged flesh

everywhere the scatter of light from the ground upwards
brilliance of dry dead things shining back in your face

great uplifted spaces glistening with blueness warm air
scent of honeyed fragrant pollens and of less sweet wax

heat smell like some soft linen's invisible cushion
the light threads of native bees, chases of flies

cicadas clicking and humming their electric shavers
a sound system hiddenly installed inside the halfway

bare dancefloor over there between the bottlebrushes
their sawing rhythm nearly as toneless as wooden clacks

but it picks up like an outboard then dies to comes back
saw-toothed that side not noticed now this side here

the great long wave of cicadas breaking like fire
night's burnt firemarks streaked down tree-boles' white flesh:

afternoon's white flesh is the memory of this
the thing which is hidden like a name is hidden

an island which is islanded because it is so far away
because it floats between skylines where distant grey trees

hover above the ground where things appear as if
in appearance they've acted on you they live they breathe

nothing is dead here the spaces between them are
inhabited leaves twigs debris fallen white-anted trunks

slopes rocks grass parrots galahs floating down
in pink streamers again the grey lack of edge

around sprays cream waterfalls of turpentines flowering
in high irrigated air-blue reaches she-oaks aspirant

with their million fingers and amber seed-flowers
spotted gums mottled as grandmothers but with contrasts

of grey brown white and silver as if dressed for a ball
the reds of the king parrot slashing the foliage

with its opening and closing flower as it flies up
vertically to land yes a blinding red and blue male

these flashes of thought these memories now planted
these hardcased seeds needing fire to sprout these nets

of dirt leaf and twig where ants fossick mason bees sandmine
these laceworks of bark litter and dropped branches

are inland floodwater you wade through to get to land
they're the fuel for the long sweep of the mind's eye

a blanket building up over the worst sterility and death
radiance offers sore bruises earth turns to clay and bakes

an imaginary tide holds blood and featherdown in flight
in place on the edge in the middle in the heart's moment

in the absent space between regions rapidly turned blue
as the ridges stretching west the gulleys sharp as razors

echo after echo after echo of a sound tracking in peaks
till it scratches small shimmers on rocks smoothed by wind

then it lays its long body out there called the west
it's the land scarcely touching the earth swarms of them

it's the land dotted with saltbrush and bush tomato
that twenty mile shadow across the claypan's a fence

which as dusk comes is a lightning-quick snake
momentarily distracting the way they appear

as if from nowhere like sentinels weathered stone
camping in that stubble sunset-toned no like mushrooms

wallabies two of them and then three over there then more
pale half-red underfur letting them melt into late light

alert as the slanting hour's alert to earth cool as wine
then the shriek as they scatter having nursed the air

having known everything as the waking dreamer
knows everything for a scattered instant instantly gone

time's far-sighted body felt beloved and lost in time
the memory of it like the memory of a lover

as familiar as a body curled around yours each day
just like when evaporating inland daybreak starts you wake

Roddy Lumsden
Stone Tape Theory

Whosoever has pushed a tear of bread
into a glossy pool of gravy
has entered history

paying the ticket price, playing statues
as they lift to their mouths
a fine brine of self,

striking the figures of those minor gods
who light the mineral tapes
of creek and cliff:

the shirtless walker raising his palm
to close out the sun's clamour
or some castaway

fetching up the cold gush to her lips
as she hangs at the stream
and a dawn hunter

dipping his thumb in a kicking breeze
to taste the *is, are, am,*
to prove the future.

Note: *stone tape theory* is a scientific explanation of ghosts which suggests
that minerals may store visual and aural information and later 'replay' it.

Emily Berry
Everything She Does Is Not Her Fault

The truth is, I didn't imagine I would melt this way,
down to my bones and my milk teeth, this old tin

I kept the things I lost in. I didn't imagine you'd
be round to see me like this, have to listen to this rattling

all night long. Darling, I don't know if you thought
about it, the way the round bone of my cheek

fits the bowl of your eye-socket exactly, the slow blink
of your still-lemonade eyes beneath my face,

each eyelash-graze a tiny sip like a bird drinking.

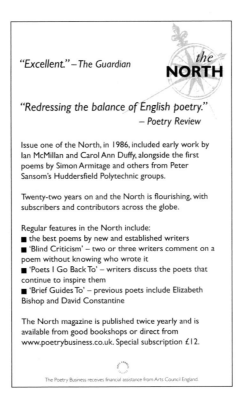

Sasha Dugdale
from Red House

Starlings in the loft and eaves of the red house
And the nestlings peep and pip at intervals, heard in rooms throughout
By the day-sick and the unfit for work. There was a golden age
For sure: there is always a golden age, like a shower of gold
Sweeter at a distance, perpendicular to the beloved body
Siring leaden times and leaden rivers. Now the madman
Calling out of his window denounces his long dead neighbours,
The starlings pass him off, stuttering, the starlings passing through –
How birdcalls make sense of sorrow and suffering
Which is subject to hyperinflation and loses its own mortal currency
In numbers. Red house, I see you in the city, on the plain
By the roadside and the railway. You are never in the mountains
Or by the sea. The smell of you is homely and nauseating
Like the smell of all humankind.

                        *

Once a man brought home a bear to the red house.
A zoo-bear, still a cub, and muzzled and harnessed.
The children were kept inside as it played. The man smoked
And twitched the reins, and ground cigarettes under his heel.
The bear snuffled under the bench and grubbed up shit and
                                        sweetwrappers.
The bear's sojourn was a gift of sorts, for the man was a romantic
And hoped his girl would relent when she saw the creature
And bring them milk in a saucer and titbits, and humanwarmth.
Until she let him in he would sleep on the landing with the bear
And teach him to dance on his hind legs, up the steps and down
In an endless manbeast cha-cha, paws clattering, feet slapping
His humming summoning succour from the stairwell.
The bear they took on the third day; it went well enough back into the
                                        light.
The man threw himself from the window, and he was lamed for life.

*

All the world is beyond the padded door of the flat.
A man once followed a girl into the red house and caught her on the
stairs.

He held a black knife in his fist, and motioned.
Others are ready for this relationship, but not her:
She reflects at length upon the imposed hostilities
She anticipates the knife pressing down on her pink skin
Until it gives, she suspects they might never be friends
Her and him, and all the while she begs and screams and whispers
Please, playing the part assigned to her with a blade's gesture.
The wrought iron design of the banisters catches her eye
It would be designed by a man, that, in its hard superfluous beauty
And knocked into place by another man, and then forgotten
Until now, until she stood and wondered: why vines and sickles and
sheaves?
Little girl, he says, I have done with this. Go now. Go. Please.

Jeri Onitskansky
The Distinct

A branch thins near the sky and ends with certainty.
In this way I move toward my death precisely.
But like the distant treetops
(each a black cloth the sky has eaten)
I occur moment by moment without distinction.
And like their vague reaching, their simple disappearance,
I stand in the wind with my hair lifting,
receiving little when standing this bare,
at once blurring and sharpening.

Alan Stubbs
A Body Of Ice Is Hot

Such a continent of white
        hands painted onto bared shoulders
                palms out-spread-fingered form angels wings
                        a place no person has been
        Or could ever have been
                when it's thirteen million eight hundred square
                                kilometres
    of ice
        water, held,
                solid celled in matrices of atoms

If you open your mouth and make a hollow
                of your cheeks
                        head swaddled in black linen
                                you can blow
            out the wind flickered candle flame
and move lines of light
        And as time passes
                lines like ropes are tricked into a face
                        onto skin
And sound washes over all, taut
            streaming as the smoke is blown

Touch the warm tight surface, rib bones lift, shoulders arch
            and in the darkness, colour
                    two people sitting at table
                        under a low light
                            drinking coffee

Reds rust, blue is electric blue, and there is an intensity of cold
            but yellows and browns illuminate this undarkness
                            and shapes play
            play into themselves, into each other
                            exploring

Sheets billow and a solo piano
                    wire taut sound- hums- as notes decay
                 making an end of themselves

And outside clouds are icebergs floating, tip visible
                 in their white-blue-sky-country above the living greens

while here in this vacuum two nipples swell to rosebuds
          and the cottages bare plaster walls become skin
                to the two bodies that lie soaking within
                       one soft cunt
                       luxuriously
                       warm and wet

Taking as much time
               cock swollen rigid
                 as they can to bathe in the glowing
                     orange light
outside of the strip light honesty
                They are
outside of the crowds
              arms raised, bodies swaying
                that rise from under music
                  to become apparent over music
                   or be within it, ears popping
                    high on atmosphere

And a sleeping bag is needed to maintain the bodies' temperature, its heat
                       even here

Out there sunlight warms skin
          and in such confusing surroundings it is impossible
            to know just where you are
               and where you end
                 and you can lose yourself
eyes closed gripping the bottom lip tight between your teeth

Should you taste blood, relax
                              warm red iron rich blood
                                        can rest to a hard clot
even though trees may guard it
            and water is released, freed, flows like the melting of a thick ice
                                                                        sheet
                              of the blue-white-Antarctic
                                        pulsing into sea

When eyes shut
            anonymous people blend into one amorphous body
                              cells, each with no purpose
                                        except to be there at this time
                                        and move together

            And what is always absent is everything else.

Kathryn Simmonds
In A Church

No, no time for this
the outside clamours to be heard,
the books, you see,
the books.
In here it's dark, the sun
has slid away.
There are necessities.
The cars are travelling at speed, without me, fast;
the days, my days, must be pinned down
accounted for and coloured in,
I need to go,
I need to go my way.

To which the soul said, *stay*.

David Grubb
What Are The Dead For?

What are the dead for?
It is to remind us not to hurry.
The poor will give us water
and those who have everything grass.
When we are not thinking the dead
dig themselves up and we can see
how tired the angels really are.
What it is to be entirely alone
in a field and feel the sky suddenly
come down.

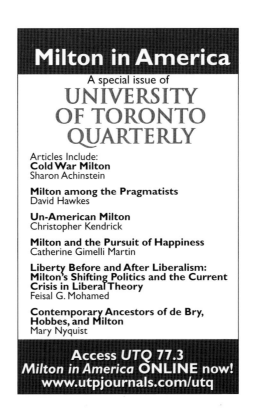

Judith Kazantzis
In Foreign Lands

That's how I like to think of you
      or how I'd choose
   to send you, wave you
sorrow's farewell at Victoria –

It would go better spun out by train,
      and after your stop
   at Paris, Milan, your boat
from Venice, Bologna, you, then

or now, manfully, expectedly,
      vanish, vanished
   along the blinding straits.
If I could twit, wind, twist, beguile

this ever clever mind, impossibly
      my sorry heart,
   then you'd leave forever,
wouldn't you, and who'd care?

Roger Moulson
The Avenue At Middelharnis

After the painting by Meindert Hobbema, National Gallery, London

The sky and trees and dusty road
invite me – though I resist sometimes –
to rest in Middelharnis.
What kind of trees they are I don't care,
I believe in them so completely,
more than those I see through my window.
I go down the avenue
towards that luminosity and the trees,
small clouds of leafage,
sway into stillness, to be true
to what the painter saw. Perhaps
he had a row with his wife
the night before he started work, and yet
its silence holds me here.

*

The painting is so clear in my mind
I shall never go to Middelharnis,
for I imagine walking up the avenue
towards the painting's distance, then turn
and see – not a road through fields –
but you and others gazing in
along the avenue to a sky
lit by the painter's desire for the world as it is
if it were clearly seen.
That sort of picture, simple perspective,
has had its time, I was told.
Yes, and its time is mine
for time has me backwards and forwards
and the days flow through me.

Peter Porter
The Vegetables At His Feet

Giordano Bruno, long affirmed in stone,
cannot remember what the spicy flames researched:
he knows alone that while the brain is brokering
its absolutes, the body's other referents
subvent a hunger, great or small,
to forge a magisterium for truth
in weak locution of our mouths and feet,
traipsing through a mortal field of flowers.

OH! MR PORTER

Poems Written For Peter Porter's
Eightieth Birthday

ॐ

John Kinsella
The Ambassadors

for Peter Porter

In cold weather we are as large
as our clothes make us, warding
off failure with diplomatic immunity,
exploring limits of the plenipotent.

We describe for our hosts the place
we come from: it's large and many
weathers threaten its coastlines. Inland
is an entirety inside an entirety,

an infinitum. An island, yet it is endless.
Yes, there is a great heat that underlies
all extremes. Yes, we retain red dust
under our fingernails years after

arriving in the Great City. Our
tastes are not lavish – we will acquire
books and tickets to the theatre,
and sack galleries for their spiritual

worth, but keep social standing
out of discussions. We *will* visit Saint Paul's
and wonder over Donne's sermons,
but no hint of Apostolic Nuncios

will haunt our office. We will offer
up raw materials, generations
of the well-fed. We will admire
the Old Country's astrologers

gazing up through smog,
bringing heaven uncomfortably
close to earth. Back home, our
skies are *so* wide and *so* shining...

we remind our hosts at moments
of triumph – Handel's 'Water Music'
on the Royal Barge, the Sex Pistols'
performance of 'God Save the Queen' –

our skies are *so* wide and *so* shining.
The embassy ends before it's begun
and yet is never complete – the skull
we bring with us shines through canvas,

our skin, and as we ascend the stairway
to hand in our resignation, the skull
comes into focus – *so* wide, *so* shining,
so willing to trade across harrowed oceans.

John Fuller
Paestum

for Peter Porter at eighty

Yesterday the sinuous Amalfi coast,
With its netted lemons the size of babies' heads;
Today a bleaker stretch towards the south,
An outpost of eleventh century Byzantium
Where a poet's hunger for eternity
Can be fairly matched by the philosopher's
Nostalgia for the accidence of birth.
The place was named for Poseidon, shape-changer,
Greedy for the bodies of boys, and is the site
Of fluted temples devoted to appeasement
Of the sea's fury and its impermanence.
We could both, couldn't we, easily visualize
That English poet who idly wandered here
In his ambition and his amorous exile?

On seeded ruins licked by scuttling lizards
(Who for a moment pause, with pale blue throats
Pulsing with life beneath their chequered green
And black) he himself in his lizardly pleasure
Paused, waistcoat unbuttoned to the sun,
To admire the mountains through the open roof
Of Neptune's temple, broken to the clouds.
At such a moment, verse is one response
To earnest glimpses of the infinite,
And ignorance the best excuse of youth.
The sea would have him soon, yawning over
His jaunty yacht, plucking with sated relish
The sodden legs, and hair, and the clutched hat,
The mountains declining his Promethean myth.

But the philosopher, for whom a glass among friends
Was the right response to an intuition of death
And who embraced it willingly in his high
Symbolic dive into that element
Which is for ever and ever changing shape,
Had long ago made his loving farewells
To talk, companionship, the search for truth;
Long ago had settled his account
With the irrelevant temples and all the little
Uncompleted tasks that filled his day;
Long ago had said good-bye to longing,
And to the sun, and to the lizard-shadowed stone;
Tucked in his head, and put his hands together
In the gesture that is both prow and prayer, – and plunged.

Les Murray
Observing The Mute Cat

Clean water in the house
but the cat laps up clay water
outside. Drinking the earth.

His pile, being perfect,
ignores the misting rain.

A charcoal Russian
he opens his mouth like other cats
and mimes a greeting mew.

At one bound top speed across
the lawn and halfway up
the zippy pear tree. Why? Branches?
Stopping puzzles him.

Eloquent of purr
or indignant tail
he politely hates to be picked up.
His human friend never does it.

He finds a voice
in the flyscreen, rattling it,
hanging cruciform on it,
all to be let in
to walk on his man.

He can fish food pellets
out of the dispenser, but waits,
preferring to be served.

A mouse he was playing
on the grass ran in under him.
Disconsolate, at last he wandered
off – and drew and fired
himself in one motion.

He is often above you
and appears where you will go.

He swallows his scent, and
discreet with his few stained birds
he carries them off to read.

Ian Duhig
The Advent Of Degree

Paranoid fantasia on a phrase from Peter Porter

Umbra Sumus

...and on the subject of the double-take,
Pale Fire's false opening made my neck ache,
not just for its bird, flying at full speed,
trying to imitate the one in Bede
which hits a windowpane it takes for air –
but how soon mis-hits glance off everywhere
from floor to ceiling, wall to nightly wall
like colours breaking on a mirrorball
around a 1960s discotheque,
and it was watching these that strained my neck.
It's strained now aping the kaleidoscope
of John Shade's poem in the style of Pope,
to focus on the "transcendental tramp"
who shoots him, and whose heart became my lamp
as I a revolutionary moth
around an ill-drawn, Asterixy Goth
who travels "marching in iambic motion",
a godless robot, lacking all emotion,
painted post-war-paranoia red.
Though Senator McCarthy's namesake said
that the book *Pale Fire*'s a Jack-in-the-box
it's many, each a nested paradox,
while Shade would use card boxes when he wrote...
we must move on but Reader, please take note.
Shade's hitman Jack – a name as often seen
for game-piece, clock-part, yob, card or machine –
was once a glassworker, whose surname Gradus
mutated into D'Argus, Leningradus;
but long before it turned into Degree,
I knew *Pale Fire* was built on Masonry –
big M, as when Shade writes 'Big G' for God,

while Mason radicals were far from odd
on Jack's dark European Continent,
and I can show these references were meant...
excuse me: I do tend to ricochet
and "Time is blood", as Chuikov would say
in Stalingradus.
                        Where did Jack's prints lead?
"Ask where's the North? At York 'tis on the Tweed,
On Tweed 'tis at the Orcades, and there
In Greenland, Zembla or the Lord knows where..."
The first time I moved North was the first time
I saw the contrapuntal art of rime,
how pale shadows were sheltering the frost
as silhouettes of trees, then all was lost
to the daylight's pedestrian translation.
Pale Fire gives Shade as "his own cancellation",
so one game or role of those being played,
casts Jack as understudy to John Shade,
the red republican one shade of Frost,
whose path with that of Jack Degree had crossed
the year of publication for *Pale Fire*,
when Cold War temperatures were getting higher;
then Frost brought Nova Zembla New World hope,
warm words from Jack, that good son of the Pope...
A man dressed as a tramp soon took a stroll
in Dallas, checking out the grassy knoll –
Pale Fire is stacked with references to chess;
we all know this, but I would like to stress
a pattern academics have ignored:
its ground-plan is the Masons' tracing board!
I know, I know: the word-count and the clock!
I'm going off at tangents and half-cock...
"Hit the road, Jack" the song goes: so did Jack;
a Shadow agent won't look back –
nor on a mission ever miss his home,
his purpose steady as a metronome –
though Mandelstam wrote "limping like a clock",
now science says there's neither tick nor tock
but alternation human brains supplied

to time's torturing drips, like stillicide
on spies whom Masons tie up under eaves.
Jack's god is Mercury, the god of thieves
science, verse, travellers, degrees and clocks.
The proper wood for carving him is box,
but Jack is less the flier than the walker –
I seem to see in him Tarkovsky's *Stalker*,
whose expeditions through his Zemblan "Zone"
in some ways seem reflections of Jack's own.
But, with Tarkovsky's father's poetry,
it's *Mirror* seems more John Shade's film to me;
that "like a fire without a shadow" line
alone's a seam some scholar ought to mine,
as that shot where the bird breaks through the glass...
but time bleeds and we have to let these pass
to get back on the road for John Shade's Wye.
There students argue: was he *meant* to die?
Do trained assassins miss their shot that near?
Whose version of this murder do we hear?
Like a made man too, Jack's motive could be
avenging Porter's sinless effigy,
that took his fall and got burnt like a witch?
Think of poet Ivan Nikolayich –
"Bezdomny", "homeless", for a nom-de-plume;
the architecture of *Pale Fire* has room.
To Masons, murdered architects makes sense.
Then there's Anxiety of Influence,
Untune That String! Bloom's paper on Degree;
but if I want to get my Ph.D.
I have to break new academic ground.
I can: the Nova Zembla I have found
is secret, ground I will be first to break...

Gwyneth Lewis
Apology To Peter Porter

Meeting you on the Underground
by chance, I gave you my seat.
I even insisted, out of respect. You,
protesting, were far too polite
to refuse and took it. My mistake.

Far better to sway like a pair of figs
maturing together on strap-hanging stems.
Though it take me a lifetime
to ripen – let's face it, we're both in decay –
like you, I'll stand every inch of the way.

Andrew Motion
The Station At Vitebsk

Our town stood on the extreme limit of the world.
At the railway station, all the trains that drew up
to platform one were returning home to Vitebsk,
and all the trains at platform two were leaving

Vitebsk. We swung between hello and goodbye
like the long brass tongue of the station clock
that never helped me answer my question: were we
living at the beginning of the world or the end of it?

The waiting room had a ceiling painted blue and gold
but the atmosphere was always tense with anxiety –
everyone was preparing to leave for somewhere else.
They might hear the bell ring three times and still

have to watch their train disappear into the distance
without them: the destination had not been announced.
All they could do then was settle down to wait again,
as if next time the Messiah would finally show himself.

My beautiful train roared, the boiler breathed flames,
and steam swallowed truck after truck of passengers.
We were travelling at last, losing the town in a cloud.
I felt I might have been going home after a funeral,

or setting out on my way to a funeral. Would there be
a place for me when I arrived, and faces I recognised?
Would the trees still be there – the deep forest I knew
and used to feel breathing on me when I was a child?

This is a 'found' poem, in the sense that it's taken almost entirely from Bella Chagall's
autobiography, *My Life* – with sections re-arranged, edited, sliced up and added-to by me.
– A.M.

Tiffany Atkinson
Another Moon Song, Rufus

for P.P.

Two, three, four –
Anyway, love's nothing
like the moon. The moon's
a drag. A passive-aggressive
in a better woman's dress. The one
you find outside your house, at 3 a.m.,
in tears, wanting to *talk things through*.
The moon has issues. She won't lighten up,
that botoxed princess who, in private, loves
to play the psycho at the high school dance –
how casually she shakes the blood from
her corsage and limps home barefoot,
smoking! Then she hacks her mama
into bits. And all day long the girl's
been starving, or a-binging, or she's
scratching at her face. And she'll
outlive us all, the chilly bitch,
she'll outlive all of us…
And *one* –

(after Catullus's Poem 34)

Sean O'Brien
Porteriana

Transported back to demi-Paradise –
Via Port Said to aid comparison –
You note down all your city's names with care,
From Bongi-Bo to Heal's and Frognal (though
You draw the line at Haslemere), likewise
The Jacobean scorch-marks left
On pages from the A to Z where miniskirts
And lycanthropes have gone in hot pursuit
Of wisdom through the bars and galleries.
The ugly rich resemble gods; the poor
Are no one but themselves; the streets are paved
With unconsoling instances, and while you work
In the high room among the holy notes,
Between the rooftops dusk stands like belief
To lead us on but not to bear our weight.
Then there are landlords to be gratified.
In time all this will help compose
The epic Bach and Arthur Mee have hinted at.
The scratches on the ceiling of the tube,
Pontormo's murdered God, those things with shears,
The whole of death and loss, are to be reconciled
In 'music's huge light irresponsibility',
When in the garden in the square the dead
Are helped into the day and spoken with afresh
Across the long white tablecloths
Where bread and wine are eagerly supplied
By teams of deaf-mute journalists and critics. There
It will be always afternoon, the taxis purring
Calmly at the gates, the oratorio delighted
To possess its soul in patience, while inside the hall
The Berlin Philharmonic longs for your arrival.

Christopher Wallace-Crabbe
Bellosguardo

for Peter Porter at eighty

Re-triggered,
I now recall
that nor-west corner
in thick heat, and
stumping along above
the Carmine
by a tread-road's
unhurried winding
and some lazy lizards
doing a late scuttle
just as I
presumably came
to his near-piazza,
one reno-villa
sprawled below me;
another leftward, higher, solid
with flame-pink
cyclamens nestled
in that umbrageous dark,
like historical truth
or the destinies
he was painfully
trying there
to unravel.

Tim Liardet
The Vipers Of Chanteau

'*...haunted by jeopardy*'
– Peter Porter

Grapevines cover our walls and hairy-bellied bees
thicken them with a second wall of humming
as if the entire house might be radioactive.
So we read and snooze, let the pages bake,
sit yawning at the white table and eat
to celebrate order – an outbreak of hands lunging.
We're safe in this place, talk fulsomely
against the sound of pollen which drips, which piles
comfort upon comfort. The hibiscus, dense with petals,
throws out in its little parody of paradise
a hundred butterflies a minute. But there are always the vipers.

They might be wrapped around the door-knob,
dozing under floorboards, or deeper down than that.
A foot might have brushed the grasses above them
and woken them abruptly, we might have passed
within a metre of them, chatting, our heavy ball thudded
a yard from their warmed coils. We don't know.
Their eyes open in sleep, a vortex of snooze,
the speed with which they might unravel and pluck at you:
all we can do is dream them, having been warned
that because they're there they do not have to make a noise;
their lack of noise does not mean they are not there.

Don't think of them, I say at the table, which sets the vipers
cutting silently through the corn-stalks of the mind.
But they're out there, we're told, don't go barefoot
into the fields for fear of treading on them
like a floor which squirms. But I have no log to throw at them,
there'll be no showdown in pyjamas and the heat
when the heat is merely itself and like a wall.
However much we trust, they observe the mysteries
and stay invisible, refuse to register anything
outside the pit of our fear or send to us
any snake-like evidence, not even the meagreest hiss, a little like God.

Alan Brownjohn
Poem For The Older Person

for Peter Porter

With an indrawn sigh, "Why is "sex" going on so long?
The columns, the pictures, the girl's song

Rock 'critics' say is 'her sexiest so far'?
It should have finished long ago. But my car

Radio (on the wrong channel) goes on yammering
About it as if sex were *new*. It's hammering

Home outdated points which the world must have learnt
Fifty years ago. Yes?"
                        I draw up, having earned

A cautious drink with this grumbling, at a place
(If you *must* know) just off the A12... I present a face

That contrives an effortful smile to a barman
Who will certainly strive to serve me, when he can,

He promises as much – but he's sorry, he has to see
To the crowd that's just come in. They're ferociously

Fond of each other, they're shabby, rich, and rowdy
(Do pity this underpaid barman... it's a crowd he

Knows well, they've come Friday night for the last
Six weeks, in their 4 by 4's... But the fad won't last.)

And they talk sex, sex, sex as they order drinks
– While this bubble in the corner floats and "thinks"

"Why is 'sex' going on so [fucking] long?"

Clive James
Peter Porter Dances To Piazzolla

First subject, *The Bank Dick*.
In the New Old Lompoc House
Fields crosses the lobby twice with the inspector.
It means the inspector fell out of the upstairs window.
In a silent film, a title would have said so:
A sound film can say it without words.

There can be word-play even in the desecration
Of an enemy's severed head.
Fulvia shoved a pin through Cicero's tongue.
What she meant was: "Where are your gibes now?"
It would have sounded better than that in Latin,
But the gesture was better still.

Harry Lime's face shifts into the light
Like the Christ of Michelangelo
Floating upward from the tomb.
Resurrection, apparition, revelation
Are among the words not used:
Nor are they by Verrocchio's St Thomas.

Garbo's Camille has drawled "Armand Duval,
Where are my *marrons glacés*?"
While still we're stunned at what she didn't say
When she turned to look at him:
She fluttered, speaking only to the eyes.
Her Queen Christina came from Samothrace.

At the luncheon on the grass
The naked woman says without a word
What must be burning in those cool men's minds,
Though the one in the white trousers might be thinking
"Sweet kid, but these green stains are going to need
Detergents that do not yet exist."

In the same way that Fields locked off the viewpoint,
The camera stays on the car
While Basil Fawlty goes to get the branch
He will beat it to death with.
No words, not even pictures of a word:
Wittgenstein, move over.

He did, the day he generously conceded,
When faced with Sraffa's Neapolitan gesture,
That its tacit content blew holes in the premise
Of the *Tractatus Logico-Philosophicus*.
A whole position had gone phut
Like the Great Dictator's globe.

Speaking of which, *A Bullet in the Ballet*
Is a great title, but you have to see it,
Because there is a letter you don't say.
See it, and you've got it to a "t".
Tell you what, let's just quit fooling around
And screw each other instead,

As Antony said to Cleopatra
At their last *bal masqué* in Alexandria.
Were the lyre, the lute, the sistra and kithara
Ever as gorgeous as what we've both just heard?
Sorry I couldn't do that last bit better,
But thank you, it was lovely and so are you.

Alan Jenkins
Remembrance In West London

to P.P.

Sunday, and the cycle-trails
Wind through smells of barbecues
From small backyards and car-boot sales
Of things that no-one wants to use
Or wear. A Bach cantata fails
And so does Art and so does booze;
Another week gone off the rails,
I haunt these grey-skied avenues
Where even cats that slink by, tails
Between their legs, seem to accuse.

Churches spill out on the streets
Their congregated pinks and mauves,
A scattering of earthly treats
Like something painted by the Fauves;
A wave of shouts and laughter greets
Each new appearance in these groves
Of souls that Jesus saved; now eats
And drinks, rotis, fishes, loaves,
Sacrificial fresh-baked meats
Await the faithful in their droves.

In rooms I glimpse through windows, dads
Are stuck with carving duty while
Ungrateful little darlings, Brads
And Britneys, semi-juvenile
And borderline-delinquent, lads
Who've learnt that violence is a style
And boy-mad girls in latest fads
Look on with a knowing smile;
Mums dream new kitchens, sofas, rads,
A Lottery-shower of cash, thick-pile.

And I am outside looking on
As always, an outcast at life's rich
And reeking feast, my chances blown –
The cheque was bad, the girl a bitch
And every moment when I shone,
A little star, is now a glitch
In the program (two-thirds gone);
I stand on stage without a stitch,
A scholar-prince without a throne,
A gentleman who sought the ditch.

When did life become this vexed,
Unhappy clinging to the past,
A frightened feeling that the next
Cigarette might be my last?
When did each book become a "text"
And good things start to go so fast
I hardly saw them? Who annexed
My script to *Dead White Male*, the cast
Grown young and cruel and oversexed,
My flag forever at half-mast?

Back home, I switch on: Whitehall
Awash with poppies, and with rain,
And berets on old heads – short, tall,
They've come by special coach or train
To step up and salute, then fall
Back in to lines that stiffly strain –
'Ten-*shun*! – while some who heard the call
Watch from their wheelchairs. Pain
And courage on lined faces, all
Live their losses through again:

Many-medalled remnant of hosts
Who fought to save us from the harm
That history threatened and the boasts
Of lunatics, so that the calm
Prosperity of Sunday roasts
And, for others, spiritual balm
Might still begin at England's coasts...
Wreaths held smartly on one arm
Some appease their comrades' ghosts
With orchid, olive, myrtle, palm:

Sons of Empire, and of slaves,
Raincoat-wearing like the others
They think of those gone to their graves,
Years that briefly made them brothers;
While, breaking over them in waves,
Sorrow for an instant smothers
Pride and comradeship, and fills the naves
Of air above them with another's
Words, they recall the guns, close shaves
And telegrams sent to mothers.

George Szirtes
Three Pontormos For Peter Porter

1. Visitation: The Burning Mothers

If only, she said, we could be born of fire
as well as die in it, if only our mothers
could be called to be flames, or be eaten
by flames and be ash like all those others;
if just once the flames could be beaten
down that burn us from within
so that we ourselves might finally retire...

I watch them flickering into life, their gowns
blown this way and that, with each child
about to be born into light and those faces
impassive as the logs that must be piled
on to keep them burning: savage graces
for ever under the bright skin,
billowing fires of burning towns.

2. Supper At Emmaus: An Empty Plate

The plate will be empty off which they must feast.
The eye of God will sort out man from beast.
The grace of God will change the nature of bread.
Wine will be blood as soon as the Son is dead.
The grace of God exists that grace might be
Lodged somewhere in creation: *gratis*, free.

3. Deposition: Discord In Colour Theory

Here it's the wind that dominates. You'll note
Those somewhat surprising colours. I combine
Them against expectation, so red, for instance,
in the form of pink, is lighter than yellow
in the form of orange. As for the blue, that sozzled
rain-dark pastel blue that seems to float
between tones so the whole thing's shrill
or gives an impression of shrillness, a dance
expressive of frenzy if you like, that billow,
that settlement of blue-grey you couldn't quite define
as blue of any one sort but leaves pink dazzled,
that's what the rest sink into or settle on,
while at the bottom the luminous figure of John,
the beloved disciple, glows, squat and still,
so light on his feet you'd not think he supports
the death of God and the wind that blows
the world awry and away so everything flows
towards a grace that elevates what it distorts.

Douglas Houston
Peter Porter Above Nant-yr-Arian, 1992

John 19:22

Your oeuvre went into orbit
The same year that Gagarin did –
Once Bitten..., 1961.
Yuri touched down within two hours,
But you never lose altitude.

The voice you are that bears you on,
Uncondescending and uncowed,
Homes on the affirmative pole,
Imagination continuous
With all the props of how we live.

The ten-tiered city rises on
Conviction's syntax spanning space
With walkway buttresses that form
The network linking discourses
In sudden contiguities.

Back then, a red kite's killer eye
Perhaps glimpsed figures on the ridge,
You gazing through the sunlit air
Across the forest stretched below
To the mountains and sky beyond.

Anthony Thwaite
Runes For Peter

Ten years ago, I mobilised your friends
(Or twenty of them) to celebrate in prose
Or verse your three-score years and ten;*
And now that decad (no final 'e') ends,
Which only shows
The difference between the "now" and "then"
Comes down to figures, meaningless and pale.
My earliest school report was plain; it said
"Anthony has no sense of number". True –
My numbering of the passing years grows stale:
Instead,
Let my "no sense of number" see us through.

* *Paeans for Peter Porter,* Bridgewater Press, 1999

CENTREFOLD

❧

Poetry, on the whole, is the most democratic of all arts: the least demanding in terms of the author's working conditions.

– Oksana Zabuzhko

His Inturned Eyes:
MacNeice In The Woods

PAUL FARLEY

Star-gazer

Forty-two years ago (to me if to no one else
The number is of some interest) it was a brilliant starry night
And the westward train was empty and had no corridors
So darting from side to side I could catch the unwonted sight
Of those almost intolerably bright
Holes, punched in the sky [...]

                          [...] which light when
It does get here may find that there is not
Anyone left alive
To run from side to side in a late night train
Admiring it and adding noughts in vain.

Recently, I took a train from London Waterloo to Sherborne in Dorset, and felt the full scale of the MacNeician planetarium. I had a copy of *The Strings Are False*, his unfinished autobiography that was passed on for safekeeping in 1941 and published after his death in 1963. There, I read a description of an incident that must have also been stored safely away:

> In January 1921 I found myself wonderfully alone in an empty
> carriage in a rocking train in the night between Waterloo and
> Sherborne. Stars on each side of me; I ran from side to side of
> the carriage checking the constellations as the train changed its
> direction. Bagfuls and bucketfuls of stars; I could open my
> mouth to the night and drink them.

There was something pleasing about the nested-ness of all these dates, of the light taking so long to arrive, so to speak, while at the same time something frustrating. I was on the same length of track, and yet the current South West Trains rolling stock don't make it easy to dart from side to side (and you'd be caught on CCTV if you did). What seemed most interesting, though, was this sense of absolute modernity and the idea of the "mobile gaze", and a sense also of sight drawing on the other senses. It reminded me of how, when I first read MacNeice, it often felt like entering both a thicket and an echo chamber.

In an essay of 1936, 'Subject in Modern Poetry', Louis MacNeice alights on the matter of "subject anxiety", one of the major literary issues of his day: "It is sometimes objected against these younger poets that their 'modern' stage-properties are a little obvious; that they introduce pylons and gasometers as automatically as older poets introduced roses and nightingales. This is often true, but it should be remembered that pylons and gasometers are not merely décor." Apart from the in-turned smile this might provoke when any youngish poet reads it – it seems there are always young poets criticized for reaching too readily for the newfangled and the immediate, and it's always intriguing looking back at the perpetually awful state of contemporary poetry – it also suggests important questions about the writer and his or her context; about the world the writer inhabits and moves through as always being a place of value and interest, regardless of age and epoch.

There was of course an anxiety concerning the journalistic and the documentary operating at this time (the 1930s). And by the end of his life, MacNeice had grown circumspect about the journalistic. But I've often wondered how much he could have imagined or foreseen a contemporary context so completely disengaged from the enormous past, either as an archive and resource, or an available panoply, as the one we find ourselves in now, where everything can seem to be happening all at once and time really is "away and somewhere else".

For poets of my generation, the year of MacNeice's death, 1963, represents something of a Year Zero, Larkin's *annus mirabilis*; though in the book he didn't quite live to see published that year, *The Burning Perch*, MacNeice is more interested in the *Magnus Annus*, Pythagoras's idea of the whole of history happening in a great year, and everything having to go round again.

The poet Peter Porter has said "we are living in the Permanent Museum, whether we like it or not", an idea perhaps corrupted by another poet, Michael Donaghy, who called our culture "a vast, posh shop with the security cameras switched off". From early on, MacNeice seems able to look in two directions at once. On the one hand, the enormous past is available to him, to be recalled and re-imagined: "It was all so unimaginably different, and all so long ago," he said, opening a tunnel that leads us all the way back to the Classical world. At the same time, his poems are also very alive to the world he inhabited, right down to the consumerist brand names and shiny surfaces that had mobilized between the wars, and whose furnishings and ethos we are still – just about – inhabiting and enduring. So we find Hamlet in the shadow of the gasworks. We get sarcophagi and celluloid. We get roses and cigarettes.

But beyond MacNeice's willingness and ability to fuse the classical and the immediate, the vernacular, to bring the past and present into interesting proximities in his poems, there lies a more interesting impulse, which concerns the question of selfhood and identity moving through the same imperfect space we all have to share, and – most interestingly, I think – what it means to see the world over and again as both a mediated thing and as a thing in itself.

If this is beginning to sound terrifyingly ontological, please relax. Writing about Malory's *Mort d'Arthur* in 1961, MacNeice described the book as "a wood which one can get lost in – but then what are woods for?" In that spirit, I'd like to look at MacNeice's poem 'Woods', which first appeared in his collection *Holes in the Sky* in 1948. Though copyright prevents, naturally, a full-scale reproduction of this poem here, it *is* in print in the *Collected Poems*.

MacNeice's father – who, we discover from another poem in *Holes in the Sky*, 'The Strand', "Kept something in him solitary and wild" – is a conduit towards a "true wild", the west. And yet, there is also this "English choice". For MacNeice, it's become almost a critical axiom to recount his betwixt and between-ness; his 'foreigner' status with an Irish readership, and his sense of 'Irish-ness' to people over the water. This sense of apartness was even broader, and not only founded along lines of nationality. As a discernible quality, it cuts right through his life on many levels, and MacNeice must have been partly complicit in presenting himself as a detached observer. At Oxford in the late 1920s, he remembered:

> … The air was full of the pansy phrase 'my dear'. I discovered
> that in Oxford homosexuality and 'intelligence', heterosexuality
> and brawn were almost inexorably paired. This left me out in the
> cold and I took to drink.

His own imaginative sense of being "out in the cold" can be examined through his poems, and it's interesting that by the time he wrote 'Woods', in the mid-nineteen-forties, he is able to manage not only a sufficient distance from his childhoods, but to hold his plural pasts in a kind of creative opposition, balancing landscape, family, myth and reading. MacNeice takes us on a walk through the woods, recalling his schooling at Sherborne by leading us into "a Dorset planting, into a dark / But gentle ambush", but as we enter the woods' enclosed space the poem suspends time, opens out, and explores the different versions of landscape available to the poet; literary, picture-book, mythical memories nested within actual memory.

The Strings Are False provides a comprehensive key to so much of this: there we can find his master at Sherborne, Littleton Powys, reading him Herrick, we can find Malory's *Morte d'Arthur* and what we'd now call 'role playing', and the little shocks of geology and topography that registered as the difference between Ireland and England. We also know that MacNeice was brought up with stories of the far West of Ireland in his ear. *In Landscapes of Childhood and Youth*, he talks about his childhood construction of dream worlds. Unlike his friend W.H Auden, who at the same time was constructing a depopulated private world made of limestone, lead mines, slag heaps and machinery (and had the textbooks to valorize it), MacNeice's consisted of places he thought were really on the map, the first of which was 'The West of Ireland':

> a phrase which still stirs me, if not like a trumpet, like a fiddle half heard through a cattle fair. My parents came from that West or, more precisely, from Connemara, and it was obvious that both of them vastly preferred it to Ulster [...]. So for many years I lived on a nostalgia for somewhere I had never been.

"A nostalgia for somewhere I had never been..." really hit home with me (if you'll pardon the atrocious pun). Growing up in Liverpool in the early 1970s, I didn't believe a place called 'England' really existed. Cricket on the village green, sunken lanes, bridleways and chalk downs were the visual fabric of picture books, but nothing I read about connected with the bin sheds and unremitting concrete and greyness outside. Later on in the same piece, MacNeice describes being sent to school in England at ten, and we get another strangely dislocating episode:

> Transported across the Irish Sea and seated in an English train [...] I kept saying to myself 'This is England' but I did not really believe it and, as it was night, could not see those differences which stamp a thing as real. But, though full of disbelief, I was vastly excited, and when daylight came I perceived that England was not just an imitation of Ireland; the fields and hedges and houses were different, and as for London when we got there [...] it was not Belfast, it was foreign. And foreign it has remained to me.

We get this sense, then, of MacNeice being twice removed from his familial source, and of also being both afloat and acutely aware of the shortfall between expectation and actuality, of being able to lever open and examine his perceptions. In 'Woods', we see a parsing of personal iconography and a way with myth that looks ahead to the poems of the late fifties and early sixties. But it strikes me mostly as a poem concerned with the difficulty of getting any access to 'the real', whatever that means. The poem's resolution – if we can call it that – leads us back into daylight – "And always we walk out again" - and into an ordered world where even the sky is framed – "An ordered open air long ruled by dyke and fence" – and lands on "inconsequent wild roses".

Mention of roses is likely to prick up the ears of any MacNeice-watcher, but again these flowers are looking ahead to later blooms. They are wildness framed, wildness neutered within a vast field of order, husbandry and tameness. They prefigure the blooms in a much later poem, 'Flower Show', published in *The Burning Perch* in 1963, where "massed brass bands of flowers" keep a man trapped in a flower show tent in their sights; these are flowers which "have long since forgotten, if they ever knew, the sky", and the only way out of this locked groove nightmare is a reconnection with flowers and their living context:

> – and now there is no way out
> Except that his inturned eyes before he falls may show him
> Some nettled orchard, tousled hedge, some garden even
> Where flowers, whether they boast or insinuate, whisper or shout,
> Still speak a living language.

'Flower Show', in *The Burning Perch*, is flanked by 'Pet Shop', and its animals taken out of a living context: "Once there was the wild, now tanks and cages", and 'In Lieu', and its "Roses with the scent bred out". If MacNeice's early poetry, from *Poems* (1935) to *Autumn Journal* (1939), accommodates the world of consumer goods, factory hooters and glossy surfaces, the later work can be said to move back into the same frames but with a renewed sense of purpose concerning authenticity and artificiality, the vitality of living variety and the deadening, distancing effects of the manufactured and the repetitive. In a way, all our perceptions of the natural world are mediated to some degree, but to get a sense of how nightmarish and enclosed the "canvas cathedral" of 'Flower Show' really is, it should be read alongside Patrick Kavanagh's 'On Reading a Book of Common Wild Flowers', published just a few years earlier: "I knew them all by eyesight long before I knew their names. We were in love before we were introduced". Like John Clare before him, Kavanagh is able to suggest an unmediated, unconditional wildness in the world; Clare famously "found the poems in the field, and only wrote them down." MacNeice's "inconsequent wild roses" are dead-headed, their wildness cancelled out by a thing called *England*.

If we really believe that MacNeice's poetry contains forces disruptive enough to work against the organizing tendencies of the canon, then it might be useful to cast the net wider and think about his work in hitherto unexamined relationships with some unusual suspects, and with that blood-chilling caveat, I wanted to think about MacNeice in the light of a poet working a century earlier, John Clare. On the face of it, the two have next to nothing in common: Clare the 'Northamptonshire peasant poet', the son of a flail thresher who was only intermittently educated, a worker in the fields around his birth home of Helpston, whose London publishers took advantage of a metropolitan vogue for rural verse that had persisted since Robert Burns; alongside Clare, MacNeice seems impossibly urban and urbane and worldly, and on the face of it the comparison would seem to suffer immediately simply because of the conflicting historical time-frames the two writers occupy, the context Clare was working in – in every sense – being so utterly removed to the one MacNeice inhabited. But, without wanting to force connections, the two writers do share something quite fundamental and important: and that is their apartness, their homelessness.

We know that Clare and John Keats came close to meeting: they shared the same London publisher – Taylor & Hessey of Fleet Street – and at their offices Keats actually scribbled a note on the nearest paper to hand, which was the back of a letter from Clare. And the two knew each other's work: when Keats was shown Clare's poem 'Solitude', he though "the Description prevailed too much over the Sentiment". And when faced with Keats's nightingale, this is what Clare had to say:

> […] he often described nature as she appeared to his fancies
> and not as he would have described her had he witnessed the
> things he described.

Clare is suspicious of Keats's allusion, the availability of the enormous past, this vast life support system of Classical mythology. (What Philip Larkin would witheringly refer to as "the myth kitty" a century and a half later.) He values firsthand experience, accurate description, the thing being described rendered faithfully from what is seen in the field, with no qualifying, intermediary apparatus. But Clare himself is only able to write following the dispersal of print culture. In fact, the discovery of books, the availability of books, precipitated a kind of crisis for Clare, albeit a crisis that generated some of his best work. Already immersed in a vernacular culture of folk song and verse, Clare's exposure to the dissemination of printed poetry – already widespread by the beginning of the nineteenth-century – provokes an engagement that will isolate and alienate him within his native culture and community. Taken to London to promote his first collection – *Poems, Descriptive of Rural Life and Scenery*, in 1820 – Clare finds himself in the fashionable drawing rooms of the metropolitan literati, and realizes he can never be a part of this. He is caught in an appalling double bind. He is "out in the cold."

A common theme is flux, and rate of change. For Clare, we might think of each microcosm going about its interconnected business, but there's an excitement and dread associated with the storms and floods that assail his landscapes, and from reading his letters as well as the poems, it's easy to imagine how contingent his situation was, especially by the 1830s. A poem such as 'The Flood' shows a part of Clare's world – the River Welland at Lolham Brigs – moving so quickly it seems to be coming apart as the river in spate dismantles and takes things away in its current:

> Trays – uptorn bushes – fence demolished rails,
> Loaded with weeds in sluggish motions, stray
> Like water monsters lost: each winds and trails
> Till near the arches – then as in afright
> It plunges – reels – and shudders out of sight.
> [...]

From very early on, MacNeice is interested in Heraclitean flow: a very early poem, 'A Cataract Conceived as the March of Corpses' from 1927, shows us a river in spate:

> The river falls and over the walls the coffins of cold funerals
> Slide deep and sleep there in the close tomb of the pool,
> And yellow waters lave the grave and pebbles pave its mortuary
> And the river horses vault and plunge with their assault and battery [...]

Thirty years later, the same concern intensifies and culminates in poems such as 'Reflections' and 'Variation on Heraclitus.'

Even though Clare and MacNeice can be said to share a kind of access-all-areas homelessness, we'd be wrong to pigeonhole the two writers as otherwise moving in entirely separate spheres of interest. You could make a case for the symmetry of their respective writing careers: after early success and critical reception, Clare's work fell out of favour and slowly slipped from view into the late 1820s and beyond, even though the poet was very much active and indeed producing some of his strongest writing; MacNeice didn't quite fall off the radar, but nevertheless the "early promise – later neglect" pattern broadly applies as he became, to use Peter MacDonald's phrase, a writer living in the shadow of "a distorted past". The 'unsophisticated' Clare, labeled and marketed as the 'peasant poet,' was capable of seeing his world through the lens of art, and producing complex, ekphrastic lyrics, for example on the work of the painter Peter de Wint. And the 'sophisticated', urbane, London-loving MacNeice was perfectly willing to rent a place in the sticks in order to get some writing done. The point's also worth making, lest any gasometers or pylons obscure our view, that MacNeice seems to have been preoccupied to a degree with the relationship between urban and rural in several early poems such as 'An Eclogue for Christmas' and 'Turf-stacks'.

In March 1946, the MacNeices had rented a house in the village of Tilty in Essex, which is where 'Woods' was probably written. It's only a few miles up the road from High Beech, and the asylum where John Clare was first treated as a voluntary patient (and from where, you'll remember, Clare walked home on foot to Northamptonshire: the famous 'flight from Essex' prose description). Here's part of a poem that Clare wrote shortly before he fled this Essex asylum:

London Versus Epping Forest

The brakes, like young stag's horns, come up in Spring,
And hide the rabbit holes and fox's den;
They crowd about the forest everywhere;
The long and holly-bush, and woods of beach,
With room enough to walk and search for flowers;
[...]
I could not bear to see the tearing plough
Root up and steal the Forest from the poor,
But leave to freedom all she loves, untamed,
The Forest walk enjoyed and loved by all!

Clare's walk through the woods, like MacNeice's, is also concerned with what's "untamed", and on first thinking about this poem I was thrilled at the thought of having maybe come across an all-too-neat analogy; especially in the way that Clare, like MacNeice, is self-consciously pulling different kinds of environments into broad contrast, even using an atypically adversarial title to signal the poem's project of comparison and estimation, a weighing up. But the more I thought on it, the more the differences overcame any tidy parallel. It isn't just that one poet uses literary allusion, or invokes a familial relationship between what's 'wild' and what's 'tame' in his idea of woods; it isn't just that the other poet looks outward more, seeing a continuum from these woods and their plant and animal inhabitants to the human world and "the poor". It's more to do with Clare's locating of "freedom" here, in the woods, because his woods begin and end in themselves, and exist in their own self-contained right. They heal themselves, conceal or shelter their inhabitants, and are openly available to all. Can we really say the same of MacNeice's woods?

It might be easy to dismiss this as a criticism of a poem not doing something its maker wasn't interested in it doing in the first place, and MacNeice's poem has other strengths anyway; and yet, I was intrigued by MacNeice's description, in *Landscapes of Childhood and Youth*, of forging a real connection between himself and his environment. At Marlborough, forced to take compulsory runs called 'sweats' against the clock through the north Wiltshire downlands and forest, he describes how:

> I loathed the conveyor belt of trees which I had to force behind me through my own leg power, and the ever-receding grey brow of the downs with their aristocratic indifference to our rainsoaked wasplike jerseys. But after a year or two of this lungs and legs became free and in pounding over the elastic earth one felt attuned to this country [...] Physical discomfort, it dawned on me, my hair one river of sweat, could be a bond between myself and my context. Or rather could help me to make a context. [...]

This chimes with Clare's own sense of significant places – the woods and fields and heaths of pre-enclosed Northamptonshire – as being able to support the work *and* the play of the people who lived there, the last of the pre-industrial English contexts supporting all manner of human and natural activity, seen and felt and experienced physically through an intimacy with landscape. Even though we acknowledge the world of difference between a public school cross-country run and a life spent working on the land.

And a world of difference, finally, between Clare's much-anthologized poem 'I Am' and MacNeice's 'I twitter Am' from the cage of his 'Budgie.' Entering MacNeice's "alluring eye" reminds me of entering the dark of a cinema, and since I first read 'Woods' I've been particularly reminded of a film that was released in the same year it was written. I hope this isn't blasphemous if only because MacNeice is so obviously open to the idea that what we've read, and what we've seen framed, materially alters the way we view and reconstruct the world – and that increasingly includes the hourly assault of images. The film I have in mind is *A Matter of Life and Death*, Powell and Pressburger's 1946 wartime love story starring David Niven and Kim Hunter, and screwing the focus even tighter, particularly that scene in which Niven and Hunter are relaxing in a Technicolor grove when there is a visitation from a heavenly emissary, who comes down to earth and enters these woods in order to stop time and speak with Niven. In the deep, rich foliage of a sound stage, our celestial emissary takes a long sniff of the rose in his buttonhole, and laments the way "we are so starved for Technicolor up there", pointing towards what I think of as a very MacNeicean concern: that shortfall between seeing things firsthand and through books and the various distorting lenses of the twentieth-century. It should also be acknowledged that this film is deeply indebted to radio, and particularly the period of experimentation that MacNeice, working for the BBC, was such a part of during the war years, especially his version of Eisenstein's *Alexander Nevsky* in 1941, which heralded a series of radiophonic verse epics.

Filters and intervening media, whether they be print, photographs, picture books or film, are only one way in which MacNeice is distanced, though, for we have to also consider ideas of childhood's unalloyed perception. Is the American poet Louise Glück correct when she wrote, in her poem 'Nostos', that "we look at the world once, in childhood. The rest is memory"? Is the first blossom always the best blossom? "The grown up hates to divorce what the child joined", MacNeice tells us in 'Woods', and the poem poses its post-Wordsworthian questions about how our engagement with the real is injured, compromised or diminished through time and ageing, and how our pasts might always be malleable, unresolved. But MacNeice never ran out of childhood. Even in the poems from *Visitations to The Burning Perch*, he is still able to mobilize memory not simply for its own sake, or to sentimentally record a loss, but to examine its securities and test its boundaries with the world.

In MacNeice's hands, there's an urgency where matters of perception are concerned; it's this dimension of his work – first encountered through 'Woods', though soon evident at all stages of his writing life – that I continue to be most excited by. What does it mean to grow up, to enter into time and consciousness, with our formative years full of broadcast music and images? How do we remember, having intimately known the microcosms of our rooms and houses and streets, but *also* the phantoms and chimeras of cinema and radio and television, while we were young, to a greater degree 'out of time' and 'living in the moment'? I've often wondered if this kind of introduction to the world is inauthentic in some way. I'd like to end by reading a beautiful but sad short lyric, terrifying actually in the way it manages to suggest to me a point in time – not so unimaginable now – when the synapses are finally connected directly via Wi-Fi to streaming (or, in spate) broadband:

To Posterity

When books have all seized up like the books in graveyards
And reading and even speaking have been replaced
By other, less difficult, media, we wonder if you
Will find in flowers and fruit the same colour and taste
They held for us for whom they were framed in words,
And will your grass be green, your sky be blue,
Or will your birds be always wingless birds?

Paul Farley delivered this piece as the second BBC Louis MacNeice Memorial Lecture, at Queen's University Belfast on 23 October 2008. His latest collection, *Field Recordings: BBC Poems 1998-2008*, is published by Donut Press in May.

ℬ

Wish you were here!

Visit the poetry society's website to find out about the Corneliu M Popescu Prize for European Poetry in Translation at www.poetrysociety.org.uk/content/competitions/popescu/ and take a journey through poetry

Half-masts: A Prosody Of Telecommunications

JOHN KINSELLA

We no longer have roots, we have aerials.
– McKenzie Wark

For some years, I divided my time between the city and the country. When I was in the city, I often used to spend time at Wireless Hill near the Swan River in the southern suburbs of Perth. It's now a recreation and nature reserve. I found this an interesting place because of the presence of native bushland in an area that had been otherwise entirely cleared, and filled with housing, but also because of its history. The Friends of Wireless Hill have noted the following on their website:

> Wireless Hill was once known as "Yagan's Lookout", providing perfect views of the surrounding area. Yagan was born in 1810 and was the son of Midgegooroo, the leader of the Beeliar tribe who were custodians of the Melville, Fremantle and Cockburn districts. Yagan was a well known figure in the early days of the Swan River colony, respected by the settlers for his strong personality and independence. He also advocated peace, believing blacks and whites could live in harmony.
>
> In 1912 the facilities at Wireless Hill enabled wireless communication to be carried out for the very first time between the east and west coasts of Australia, between the mainland of Australia and shipping up to 1,600km into the Indian and Southern Oceans, and between Australia and the rest of the world.
> (http://www.sercul.org.au/wirelesshill.htm)

In this simplistic and hebephrenic account of "Yagan's Lookout" (Yagan was murdered and beheaded by white youths) we see a typical absorption of indigenous presence through assimilation into a white timeline. Wireless Hill, as we find in the second paragraph, was an extremely significant telecommunications site through to the 1960s. Not only did it allow for the first contact between east and west, but it was a key point in military communications for that period, so the suburban enclave became a radiating centre of State. The most distinctive features of the landscape, on top of the hill, were three massive concrete towers which had anchored the giant aerial. During my early visits, all that was present apart from these towers was a small telecommunications museum and a moderate-size aerial used by amateur wireless operators. A more recent visit brought the shock of a huge mobile telephone tower emanating high amounts of electromagnetic radiation. Next to this is a children's playground and a picnic area.

These paragraphs from the Friends of Wireless Hill website make an unconscious (I suspect) colonisation of indigeneity into the history of occupation of airspace with radio and other waves. Not only has the land been taken – its earlier pre-colonial status strangely emphasised by the fact of the remaining bushland as an island among the larger visual overlay of suburbia – but as far as the eye can see, and you can certainly see a long way from up on Wireless Hill, is occupied vertically as well as horizontally by the emanations and receptions configured by the telecommunications mast.

Radiation is rhythmic. Telecommunications are textual. The combination makes for a prosody, a theory of versification that is colonising and in the end destructive. This destruction too is rhythmic. Tetrawatch in the UK, a research-based campaign against the detrimental effects of Tetra mast radiation, tells us on its website:

> [...] TETRA masts pulse at 70.56Hz (4 x 17.64). However, in this pattern the first and last pulses are not separated, so there is a steady rhythm 'di-di-dah-di-di-dah', 17.64 times a second. The music of TETRA? Our bodies recognise patterns and rhythms and frequencies exceptionally well: this is not raw energy, it is information to us, interfering with our own informational bioelectromagnetic systems.
> (http://www.tetrawatch.net/tetra/pulse.php)

Of course, as poets we will recognise the *di-di-dah* as an anapaest, and will immediately interpret these rhythmic possibilities as forms of poems. The hearing of a poem, as we know, operates on many levels: the pleasure of the experience of hearing does not mean that we haven't undergone some kind of psychological shift that we are unaware of, and which could be positive or negative. So it is with the radiation of telecommunications. Ironically, as we stand within the vicinity of mobile base stations, or indeed use mobile phone technology (which I don't), we are converting through speech and text innumerable "sound poems" which we can't see but which can be registered scientifically as pulses. So our words, whatever they might be, also carry a different kind of sound we don't necessarily hear.

When I spent time in my early years at Wireless Hill it was often with my young first son on access visits, having been separated from his mother. I went there because of the mixture of bush, which I love, and general recreational facilities. I wouldn't do that now. Unsurprisingly, when I wrote poems out of these visits, I wrote not only of the disjunction between the natural environment, the history of telecommunications, and the realm of suburbia that surrounded it all, but a history of the unseen yet prosodic waves that had filled the atmosphere around this area and echoing out.

One such poem was entitled 'Wireless Hill', and the relevant stanzas concerning the unseen textuality of conversation, went:

>   And from
>   the central tower I look out over
>
>   Alfred Cove, and absorb the river.
>   You watch the children ski down slides
>   in the adventure playground and scoot
>
>   their bikes about the walkways, the sticky
>   hum that comes with rubber on hot concrete
>   reminding you of our son. You look
>
>   to the base of the tower, I look out –
>   even further than the river. But the sun
>   drives us toward the shade and touching
>
>   earth we hear the silent conversations
>   that crackle so faintly, too faint even
>   for aerials to detect.

Where I live with my current partner and children now, at the gateway to the central wheatbelt in the Avon Valley of Western Australia, we are surrounded by low-lying, eroded hills that were once the core of the Dyott mountain range. Directly behind our house is Walwalinj or Mount Bakewell, the highest point in the wheatbelt. Throughout the wheatbelt, the highest points are crowned by telecommunications masts. Being the highest point, Walwalinj is particularly encumbered with such apparatuses. Stories in town go back thirty years about old-timers wanting to fix them with a stick of gelignite. That was when the main tower primarily looked after television, radio and police communications. There is also an aircraft beacon up there, used by the military. In the last few years, mobile phone and wireless technology base stations have been added up there.

Our son Tim looks out of his bedroom window onto the beauty of the mountain, and its corruption in the form of telecommunications towers. As with most high places in the wheatbelt, it was where explorers, in this case Ensign Dale, surveyed the land below and in essence laid claim to it for the Crown. In the same way that Yagan's Lookout becomes an historic euphemism for the attempt to "blind" the traditional owners of the land, so too does Walwalinj, or Mount Bakewell, as Ensign Dale named it, establish a point of surveillance from a sacred indigenous place. The telecommunications towers are the acme of that surveillance and occupation.

The phantom egalitarianism of telephonic exchange: the ordinary citizen sends messages to the tower as much as receives them, and private industry has staked its airspace, its radiation space, though in fact it is still mediated and controlled through the rules and regulations of the State. Its claims are vertical and horizontal. Its claims are the shape of poems. In order to placate then four-year-old Tim, whose fear of these masts is almost fantastical, we offered to drive him round the back of the mountain so he could see them from the other side, because he thought they were monsters. At the time I was working on the Inferno canticle of my "distraction" of Dante's *Divine Comedy*, and it was inevitable that this experience would work its way into the text. Here is the end result:

Anti-clockwise Canto of the Moebius Strip: back of Walwalinj – "the mountain" (Inferno 34)

So Tim has seen the back of the mountain,
asking us to turn back home in case we end up
any closer to the communications masts

than we already live. We drive through
the passageway where Satan-legs wave
like tendrils of cloud, and farm dams

look so suspicious that Tracy and I
spell things out: "have you noticed how
much dead oats swirled about around

the mouth of farm dams look like p-u-b-i-c
hair...". Be careful, he's learning
to spell fast. Tim's fear of the back

of beyond might have something...
an extra antenna is visible, having gone
up unseen over the last year.

On Walwalinj, with its powerful spirit,
a devastating energy whips and lassoes.
At home, Tim draws roads snaking

about mountain on which red masts
bristle. He draws them from every angle:
an exact science, a diorama
     of love and loss.

There are only fragments of the original bushland left in the Western Australian wheatbelt. Many of the reserves that remain are small, and are ultimately collapsing ecologies because of lacking corridors connecting them to other remnants. Quite a number of these small reserves are on comparatively high ground which, being targeted by telecommunications personnel as ideal locations for their masts or towers, are inevitably damaged, not only by the radiation from these structures but also through the sheer act of installing and maintaining the equipment.

We live about 800 metres or perhaps a kilometre from these masts. When the wireless technology was installed, I wrote to the company complaining about the risk they were putting my family, especially my children, at. These were the questions I put to them:

> 1. Did you clear or damage any bush on mount bakewell installing your tower?
> 2. What assurances can you give locals re health issues pertaining to emissions from the tower?
> 3. Why wasn't there public consultation about its installation?

Their reply was polite but said that their installation complied with national standards and was completely safe. I challenged that with a series of data from investigations done in the USA and the UK, which clearly showed evidence for their safety was in the least inconclusive. This time I received no reply.

In writing this place, its ecology and its histories, which are tormented and sanitised in the way they are conveyed, not only to visitors but to many of the people who live here, I am constantly confronted with the visual aspect of these telecommunications masts, and the knowledge that their language, their poison, is written all around me unseen. One can write about wandoo trees, or marri crown decline on Walwalinj, but not to mention the communications masts would be an error of both fact and aesthetics. Bizarrely, there exists a practice in some places of disguising mobile phone towers by making them either look like vegetation, specifically trees and palms, or even masking them entirely in these forms.

I have long been protesting against not only mobile phone base stations, whether they are in country areas or clustered next to dense housing, or hospitals, or hotels, in the city, but also against the possible health risks of the actual phones themselves. More recently, I have extended this to wireless internet technology with its deplorable colonisation of public and private spaces, with so-called "hot spots". This is language that bends itself without much difficulty to poetry, but references alone to potential problems with this technology, do not make a poem an activist poem. What does?

In travelling through the wheatbelt and mapping the lines of connection between telecommunications masts, one is writing a map not only of technology but also of uncommunication. Recently my mother asked a telecom representative about the safety of birds and other creatures around the telecommunications mast up on Walwalinj. The short, sharp reply came: "Well, if the birds perch on some of that communication equipment, they're fried." Whether this is truth or exaggeration, much evidence exists that wildlife as well as humans suffers.

These artificial "trees" these potential roosting and perching places, become zones of death. Gaston Bachelard, in *Air and Dreams: An Essay on the Imagination of Movement*, asks:

> What is the bird doing on the great stone tree? Is he not adding his wing to motionless height? Rigid treetops are not entirely aerial. The dynamic imagination wants everything in the heights to move.[1]

If the imagination compels us to make the stilled move, if we are compelled to communicate, there is an unresolvable contradiction in these "trees"

1. Gaston Bachelard, trans. E. R. & C. F. Farrell, *Air and Dreams: An Essay on the Imagination of Movement*, The Dallas Institute Publications, 1988, p.210.

whose movement is damage. The story of Babel, in which the tongues of the workers were confused and no single language was the same, was a result of hubris. Discussing mobile mast towers in this light easily becomes humorous or bathetic, because we don't usually see the consequences; because there is no immediacy, there is irony.

> There is an entire poetics of trees as both vertical and horizontal entities. The vertical is obvious, but the horizontal is visually defined in branch structures, and also in the unseen root structures. In a sense these telecommunications masts and towers function as simulacra of trees on high places (one might think of the "high places" of the Hebrew scriptures), as altars of exchange. These steel structures barely move in even the strongest storm. The trees around them, whipped to a frenzy, seem to be where all motion is. But ironically, in the electromagnetic activity, these steel structures are constantly in a state of stormy activity. It's easy slippage into Bachelard's words from here: "In a storm, too, the tree, like a sensitive antenna, sets the dramatic life of the plain into motion."[2]

The spiritual colonisation of what is now known as the wheatbelt has long concerned me. As a child attending church services in the oldest inland church in Western Australia – its belltower cracked by the Meckering earthquake in 1968 – I became aware of the disjunction between the ideas of place I'd received through farmers' recounting of indigenous "stories" and the teachings in church of land, especially in Isaiah and Ezekiel, that belonged to an entirely different landscape. However, in my head, without a political knowledge of the problems associated with doing so, I merged the two.

As a poet in adult life, with committed views on land rights and respect for the intactness of cultural coordinates outside my own, I can only deconstruct this conflation. Walwalinj is a very sacred place to the Balardong-Nyungar people. Yet they are entirely cut off from access due to the nature and telecommunications reserves being surrounded by farmland. Paragliding clubs have greater ease of access through private dealings with landowners than the Balardong-Nyungar community.

When I write about the mountain out of our back door, all of these factors necessarily inform my interpretations of this place. The corruption of

---

2. Bachelard, p.216.

access for traditional people seems to me to go hand-in-hand with the poison, the radiating, of the entire environment and atmosphere around the mountain's summit. The poem that follows, though written about an icon painted by the great contemporary Russian icon-painter, Alexander Deriev, is about all of these issues.

Isaiah Icon

Woe to you who add house to house
and join field to field
till no space is left
and you live alone in the land.
– Isaiah 5:8

The Mount Bakewell Conservation Park.
    Walwalinj Conservation Park.
   Both have a certain
    kind of ring to them:
as names, as possibilities.

These are not socially conscious
    reviews of landscape,
   but right-on-the-edge
    resistances as the woe
comes to the besieged

flora and fauna, the wheatbelt
    alpine orchid that exists
  only up there, a strong
    stone's throw away.

The farmers are joining
    paddocks; the recreationalists –
paragliders, climbers, shooters –
    are joining erosions that supplant
in place of trees, flowering plants,

kangaroos, golden whistlers, parrots;
    building out like the trend
  for country living,
    an end in itself,
a means of resolution;

alone with the quarry,
  alone with the bird's eye view
 of a distant neighbour's little white lies,
  alone with a contemplation
of spaces in the body

closing in, filling out,
  the run-together thoughts
 blurring profit and loss,
  cancer cells setting off
biopsy alarm bells,

the ring of fate and damnation
  and claustrophobic interiors
 of conservation out of reach
  of the wanderer, the tourists...

I have already mentioned the obvious link between the telecommunications masts and trees. Taking the scriptural theme one more step, one might think of the Asherah poles, compared to, or planted beside trees, of Kings and other books of the Hebrew writings; these poles appeared on many high places and were condemned by the God of the Israelites because they pertained to a rival religion. I allude to this by way of demonstrating a long-standing Judaeo-Christian cultural concern with a particular image of verticality. In the context of the primarily Christian colonisation of this region, this seems somewhat ironical in the least. Furthermore, at Easter each year in this town, and permanently in Pingelly, another wheatbelt town, huge metal crosses are erected on local hills as a kind of symbolic telecommunication of the Passion of Christ. I have also written poems, unsurprisingly, about this phenomenon. The Cross is also known as the "tree".

Bachelard, talking of the image of the tree and verticality, tells us that:

> from this vertical life, the most diverse imaginations, whether they be of fire, water, earth, or air, can relive their favourite themes. Some, like Schopenhauer, dream of the pine tree's subterranean life. Others, of the wind and the angry rustling of pine needles [...].
>
> [...] Thus a single object can give "the total spectrum" of material imaginations. The most disparate dreams cluster

around a single material image. It is even more striking to think that these disparate dreams, before a tall, upright tree give themselves over to a certain orientation. Vertical psychology imposes its primary image.[3]

There are many tangents that one might take from this point of departure, whether it be looking at Roberto Juarroz's 'Vertical Poetry' as vertical textuality, or poems on trees, or human-made structures that resemble, mimic or replace trees. There are also individual poems such as Plath's 'I Am Vertical' in which the vertical is public and susceptible to scrutiny, and the horizontal becomes the private and the hidden. Or even, indeed, thinking of mimesis, how verticals constructed in particular patterns, such as telecommunications masts interlinking across the wheatbelt, mimic processions or progressions in various religious or social rituals. Eric Auerbach, in *Mimesis: The Representation of Reality in Western Literature*, says:

> Many realistic forms – the Dance of Death for example – have the character of processions or parades. The traditionalism of the serious, creatural realism of this period [the Middle Ages] is explained by its origin. It stems from Christian figuralism and takes almost all its intellectual and artistic motifs from the Christian tradition.[4]

I wish to reiterate that in highlighting these possible connections, I am attempting to critique the interference and overlays of a colonising process, and not to add to them.

Trees, as mentioned earlier, are both vertical and horizontal at the same time. Another association, that between the tree and the gallows, is reiterated in Bruce Dawe's poem 'A Victorian Hangman Tells His Love':

> This noose
> with which we're wed is something of an heirloom, the last three
> members of our holy family were wed with it, the softwood beam
> it hangs from like a lover's tree notched with their weight.

This horrifying image represents the gallows as communication device not only in its public warning but also in the intimate conversation between those

3. Bachelard, p.205.
4. Eric Auerbach, *Mimesis: The Representation of Reality in Western Literature*, Princeton University Press, 2003, p.247.

who are united in the death it brings. (The death sentence wasn't actually taken from all Australia's law books until 1985, though the last hanging was in 1967.)

If the associations I am making seem tenuous, it is worth noting that defenders of mobile phone technology insist that radiation from these towers travels primarily horizontally, on a slight slope, with relatively little threat to those immediately below, but recognising that the point where the beam reaches the ground there is a vulnerability. The whole issue of what constitutes verticals and horizontals is strongly intertwined with the rhythm of the signals themselves, forming an array of vertical stanzas with complex linearity across the landscape functioning as field of the page.

There is no escaping vulnerability, and many people will respond by pointing out that if it's not the radiation from phone towers that gets us, it'll be something else. Apart from being a cop-out on a personal level, this attitude suits market capitalism and the State, and is a self-fulfilling prophecy, or even an evocation of immunity from having to worry about the effect of our consumer lives on "nature". In discussing these issues, my partner Tracy reminds me of Geoff Page's poem, 'Out There', in which the reader can't really tell whether the speaking voice is holding a particular view or satirising it, when it says:

> I've seen what's out there way beyond
> the city lights and cars
>
> that flow like complex sentences
> too difficult to parse.
> I love the carbon compromise,
> the smell of coffee bars.

Tracy also brings to my attention Margaret Atwood's lines from *Power Politics*, in a poem discussing Western social (post-)modern estrangement of humans from 'nature': "Do you want to be illiterate? / This is the way it is, get used to it."

Constant questions of vulnerability and anxiety are in fact protections against corporate or State entities that would exploit us for their profit. The cyborg acceptance of vulnerability, as opposed to intactness of "self", runs the risk of complicit with the State and its corporate extensions/supports.

Donna Haraway writes:

> Immunity and invulnerability are intersecting concepts, a matter
> of consequence in a nuclear culture unable to accommodate the
> experience of death and finitude within available liberal
> discourse on the collective and personal individual. Life is a

window of vulnerability. It seems a mistake to close it.[5]

We hide behind these post-modern myths of vulnerability and ambiguity, and what we in fact most desire in poetry are these qualities as well, in order to allow for alternative and subtextual readings that provide for the agency and individuality of the reader. I have long defended this myself: that is, the recognition that a poem does not read the same for one person, in one place in one context, as it would for others in different places and contexts. However, if one is considering a poetics of activist outcomes, in which the very prosody of the poem itself reflects upon and reflects those *politics of outcome*, then one has to consider exactly what these ambiguities and vulnerabilities might mean. Do we value the aesthetic over the desired activist outcome? Or is aesthetics in fact merely an adornment to attract as wide a range of readers to the 'cause' as is possible? Of course I am getting into very dangerous territory here, but I do believe that a desired activist outcome is not a diminution of the possibilities of a poetic text to be moving, informative and intellectually challenging, by being specific in its aims. Contrary to what Haraway says, the bombardment of the pleasures of the text (these are obviously not Haraway's words) and maybe by extension the creation of the cyborg-poem which incorporates both the flesh of the body and the technology that allows it to be recorded and transferred (from printing press through to text messaging through to the internet) is a myth: there is a cost involved in all of this. Of course life does have a cost, but a consciousness of minimising this cost should be part of how and why we constitute our poems, and certainly how we convey them to our audiences.

It seems to me that the logical extension of Haraway's and others' arguments is to intersect with those of hybrid artists working with biotechnology. The living becomes expedient in the process of creating an aesthetic. An example of this practice is to be found in the SymbioticA research laboratory at the University of Western Australia: where you can in fact do a Master of Science in Biological Arts (doing "creative bioresearch"). That can entail an entire subversion of scientific ethics, even, to make use of living organisms to convey artistic messages. Poetry and text are always favourite transferences, utilising vehicles such as skin or other body parts, human or otherwise. If you don't see much of a gap between this and using paper (and we have to be conscious of our usage here too), then there are at least two levels of scrutiny to consider. The first is the abuse of the rights of

---

5. Donna Haraway, *Simians, Cyborgs and Women: The Reinvention of Nature*, Free Association Books, 1991, p.224.

the animals, for example, involved themselves, and second, the issue of torture. The use of living animals clearly fits into this category. Probably the most famous example of what might concern us when talking about the ethics of usage and manipulation of living organisms for so-called "artistic purposes" is the transgenic "bunny" engineered by Eduardo Kac:

> GFP Bunny (2000) – With GFP Bunny Kac welcomes Alba, the green fluorescent rabbit, and explains that transgenic art must be created 'with great care, with acknowledgment of the complex issues at the core of the work and, above all, with a commitment to respect, nurture, and love the life thus created.' The first phase of the GFP Bunny project was completed in February 2000 with the birth of 'Alba' in Jouy-en-Josas, France. The second phase is the ongoing debate, which started with the first public announcement of Alba's birth, made by Kac in the context of the Planet Work conference, in San Francisco, on May 14, 2000. The third phase will take place when the bunny comes home to Chicago, becoming part of Kac's family and living with him from that point on.
> (www.ekac.org/transgenicindex.html)

If you're wondering what the connection is between this work of "art" and poetry: I first came across Kac's work in a poetry journal, *The Notre Dame Review*, which carried his 'Biopoetry', which I will get to shortly. Before that, though, to emphasise an interconnectedness between the various issues I have been tracing here, it is worth knowing that Kac has also been eminent in the field of so-called Telecommunications Art in the pre-internet era. In his short poetics piece, 'Biopoetry', published in *NDR* Winter 2005, and about which I wrote to the journal's editors asking for a right of reply, receiving a vague "maybe", Kac includes such proposals as "Microbot performance":

> Write and perform with a microrobot in the language of the bees, for a bee audience, in a semi-functional, semi-fictional dance... The 'robeet' (robotic bee) would allow a poet to write a performative dance-text that has no reference in the physical world (that is, does not send bees in search of food). Instead, the new choreo-graphy (kinotation) would be (bee) its own reference. (145)

This proposed interference in the communications between bees calls to mind recent speculation (the research is not conclusive) that electromagnetic radiation might well contribute to the Colony Collapse Disorder, with loss of bee population, that is spreading through North America and some parts of Europe (http://www.independent.co.uk/environment/nature/are-mobile-phones-wiping-out-our-bees-444768.html). This speculation has been strongly challenged since the research did not in any way prove that mobile phones or their base stations cause the bees to desert their hives; the researchers, in a limited study, merely tested the effect upon bees of DECT (digital cordless phone) radiation. However, the attempt to create a poetics out of communication/miscommunication is clearly anthropocentric and self-serving; it's unlikely to have the bees' interest (and the interest of an ecosystem that depends on them) at heart.

When I was twenty-four, I wrote a poem entitled, 'The Dance Movement of Bees', which included these lines:

> bees cluster
> in the half light
> unable to decipher
> a river broken by ferries,
> the tightening railway tracks,
> the blurring of bridges
> and skyscrapers,
> the diminished scents
> of shrinking flowers
> (*Night Parrots*, 1989)

Another proposal from Eduardo Kac's Biopoetry manifesto is "interaction" (or interference?):

> Marine mammal dialogical interaction: compose sound text
> by manipulating recorded parameters of pitch and frequency
> of dolphin communication, for a dolphin audience. Observe
> how a whale audience responds and vice-versa. (p.145)

This seems overtly abusive when there is considered speculation on the way in which sound can distress cetaceans, possibly even to the point of self-stranding and death, and when we know so little about how this happens. Kac's proposal constitutes a poetics of abuse or in the least, a poetics of curiosity and entertainment. Communication that seeks to oppress and control is rightly identified in human discourse as reprehensible, even in such cases where coercion is used to elicit information for example on potential 'terrorist' activities. But there is little to protect animals outside shady self-serving animal welfare regulations, which are always open to interpretation anyway, and in the case of many universities are subject to little more than committee-based interpretation and enforcement.

A. D. Hope, in his empathetic and sympathetic poem 'The Cetaceans', appropriately pinpoints the issue. The final stanza reads:

> And so, too late perhaps, since in the past
> We killed all minds that might have matched our own,
> Now we turn desperately to this last
> Cradle of kind and hope from the unknown,
> Outcasts from life, self-doomed to be outcast,
> Crying: 'Comfort us, speak to us, say we are not alone,
> Cherish us in the wilderness we have made
> And where we wander unfriended and afraid'.

We might extrapolate from this that a desire to communicate with the cetaceans substitutes for a desire to affirm our own necessity having so often destroyed the other side of a given conversation. I believe Kac and artists of his ilk are often seeking to validate their own subjectivity by constantly finding other sides of a conversation that won't necessarily challenge them. That is, a conversation on their own terms.

Artists/poets such as Kac use science only in so far as it serves their curiosity and artistic utility. Poetry easily attaches itself to the pseudo-science in its anxiety to find relevance to and a readership in a changing world. This brings to mind the whole notion of risk and anxiety – that which we are prepared to up with in order to enjoy the so-called benefits of modern living. Mobile phones fit this category. In his book of essays *The Perception of Risk*, Paul Slovic tells us:

> Citizens of modern industrial societies are today learning a harsh and discomforting lesson – that the benefits from technology must be paid for not only with money but with lives [...] Every technological advance carries some risk of adverse side effects.
>
> Reduction of risk typically entails reduction of benefit, thus posing serious dilemmas for society.[6]

---

6. Paul Slovic, *The Perception of Risk*, Earthscan, 2000, p.80.

Slovic, whose concerns are for policy and how it reacts to issues of technological risk, notes that policy-makers undertake "risk-benefit analysis", "an offshoot of cost-benefit analysis".

The model in the end always boils down to the benefits outweighing the risk. These risks, though, are not necessarily measurable in the short-term and though something like mobile phones can be termed the "new asbestosis" or the "new nicotine" time-bomb, the claim of not only benefits, but of necessity, of inseparability from modern life, allows for incredible leeway regarding potential damage to people and environment. (Yet it was only a few years ago that people managed unknowingly without mobile phone technology or wireless internet.) So we observe terms emerging such as "precautionary principle", "prudent avoidance principle", "ALARA (as low as reasonably achievable)" etc.

So where does this leave us as poets and activists? I have tried to show that there is a physical link between the new technologies of communication and the writing and conveyance of poetry. These links may seem tenuous, but when you consider that you are using your phones and computers constantly both to write and to convey your poetry, and that the rhythms of typing and texting and even attaching documents will affect how and what you write, it's not as distant as it might seem on the surface. In the case of poets writing landscapes in which these towers become tree become text, it is a material fact.

If you are interested in the damage not only towers but mobile phones themselves do to humans and other living things, the research is abundant and it is not my purpose here to prove it wrong or right. It is my purpose to bring attention to the fact that our liberties are only "allowed" in so far as they benefit or profit the corporate State. (The corporate State can be Marxist as much as it can be "democratic".)

We may not all feel that the most effective form of direct action is to take a tank to ram down mobile phone towers, as one man, a former Telstra worker, reportedly did in 2007, allegedly because of radiation poisoning received while working around the towers. However, by abandoning the technology, we would allow it to die the unnatural death it deserves. There are other prosodies that we can't see in the atmosphere that have long been with us and that we might tap into instead. I'll leave them to your imagination.

John Kinsella's latest collection, *Shades of the Sublime and Beautiful*, is published by Picador.

℘

The Whale Butchers

TOM LOWENSTEIN

This episode is extracted from a longer narrative of the 1976 whale hunt at Tikigaq, Alaska, when Suluk and Artemis, a married couple in their mid-thirties, capture a bowhead whale and Suluk's crew brings it to be cut up on the land-fast sea ice and distributed.

Inupiaq Eskimo words:
umiaq – a skinboat
umialik – male or female boat owner
Qalgi – quasi-ceremonial grouping
Tulugaq – raven; originally the whale hunting trickster, Tulungigraq
maktak and *tirragiik* – whale skin with blubber attached
'The Three Muses' are a group of teenaged girls

After the harpooning, there is an interlude of dazed anticipation. We stand through the small hours gazing from the land-fast ice until finally a smudge appears on the western horizon and twelve hours later four skinboats labour to the ice edge dragging towards us their thirty tons of Suluk's bowhead. Last week, I witnessed a scene on an even more exalted scale, when three whales were harpooned in quick succession. It was misty twilight when the news came and I sledded to the site, arriving one hour later, my bones in a jumble, three miles south of our camp.

A vast plateau of ice had been marked out by four tents, their chimneys smoking in a light north wind. It was three in the morning, and sloping across a pale grey sky were banks of dishevelled strato-cirrus. Silently moving across the snow-field came dozens of women and children who had left the village in the early morning to take part in the butchering. Fixed above them to jointed harpoon-shafts, streamed three Old Glories, one for each whale, in faded cotton, kept by whale boat owning families from the patriotic 1940s. The scene was unearthly, pregnant with apocalypse, and as though emerging from some battle at the end of time, *the folke stoode amayzed this glouryous morninge, wayting for their captaine's signalle...* We dreamily idled till the women had lit fires and boiled *tirragiik*: a large slab from the whale's back which each of us ate in violent quantities, plastering each segment of floppy black skin and its grey wad of fat with mustard or ketchup. I spent the forty hours that followed with my gloves half-frozen to the oil and salt drenched ropes with which we winched the three whales from the sea, and the hacked meat into blubber-cased parcels for transport to the village.

Back at Suluk's we stand peering at our fish. Suluk is stunned by light reflected from the ice and long hours on the water. But now he must decide where to do the butchering. He must also get help from other crews and assemble equipment: block and tackle, flensing knives and ropes and sleds. He also needs an older man to supervise the distribution.

Suluk's sudden and imperative solemnity is *irigii* (frightening). As he limps up the ice towards the tent, he emanates a weary and unwilling heroism. He walks with his head down. He cannot, for the moment, in the light of his good fortune, look at us. We are too far removed from the realm he's entered. But modesty requires, at the same time, that he struggle with hubris.

The great hunters in old village stories radiated this same mix of pride and self-effacement. To bring in a whale was the sublime achievement: but it made you vulnerable to rival hunters and jealous shamans. To counter this exposure, the *umialiks* affected modesty and reticence. They moved slowly, spoke little. From season to season, and with each new whale, their reserve grew more stately. This tension between a suddenly acquired power and self-governing humility generated two ecstatic moments. The first came after the harpooning. Alone with his skinboat crew, the *umialik* allowed himself a shout of triumph, an arrogant cry: a whooping diphthong, "*Ui! Ui!*", like a seal's bark, clipped off at the teeth an octave higher than its starting register. Insolently belched, with no audience beyond the crewmen, it addresses the soul of the dead whale and the spirit of the moon which made the whale's capture possible – and likewise to the cosmos which the moon controls, and in which the *umialik* has established a new position. Further exalting his triumph, the *umialik* took a raven-skin from a bag of amulets that he kept under his bench, and opening the wings, laid it over his shoulders so the head and beak nodded over his forehead. At this moment, he becomes Tulunigraq, the Raven Trickster who created the village from the Ur-whale of mythology.

The joy-shout is repeated in the skin-toss game that marks the end of the whaling season. This is his second moment – soaring with his wife on the seal-skin blanket which had covered his whale-boat – of release and transcendence. Again transformed into the Raven, the *umialik* flies to proclaim the same ascendance. Exuberance must otherwise drum on the mind-mask's inner tissue, as he bends his persona, season by season, to more impenetrable levels of gravity.

Suluk's limp reinforces my sense of his ambivalence. I am familiar with his arthritis: any moment now, he'll ask me for some Tylenol. Now as he walks towards us, I'm aware of another wound. Suluk has killed a whale. But he, too, is symbolically wounded, and our happiness for him is clouded with protectiveness and fear. Having gone out humbly in his skinboat, Suluk has returned with a semi-divine aura, which he and his wife must express with a knowledgeable generosity and studious denial of hubris. Old stories of feuding long attested pride and selfishness. How vulnerable Suluk seems, therefore, as he limps towards us: as though balancing judiciously the filament of light that surrounds him over a vacuum which separates it from the body, and to which, as the community projects it, it should cling. One false move, and this gilding will slip into the air, leaving the *umialik* naked in his Sears Roebuck parka.

Suluk reaches the sled and rummages for a pole-knife. He murmurs a self-deprecating joke. We, uncelebrated, smaller, people maintain our silence as he limps back to the water to mark the whale's skin for the extraction of *tirragiik*. The whale lolls flexibly in the current, awaiting dismemberment. The grind of Suluk's one boot, and the drag of the other, suggests how painfully he is tethered to the creature he's brought in. The whale is his, his wife's, his crew's, his *qalgi*'s and the village's. It has left its own tribe and agreed to enter the world of the human. But Suluk must mediate all these connections: and this other-species-blood-brotherhood, tying him to the whale and demanding that their connection flow into every branch of Tikigaq society, is awe-inspiring and oppressive.

I glance at the tent we have by now set up and filled with floorboards, boxes of food, skins, stoves, bags of clothing. One of the Three Muses lights moss and dried spindrift and starts feeding blubber into the half barrel camp stove I'd helped Suluk cut in the winter. As Suluk passes, he turns, and with an ambiguous gesture, calls out, "Move the tent!" His voice is toneless; it comes from a strange distance, capricious but urgent. For the next two hours we sullenly drag camp thirty paces south. I'm ferociously hungry, freezing, sweat-soaked. When someone offers me a swig of Pepsi, it cascades down the throat in a glacier of caramel.

A long wait follows while Suluk's news travels along the ice to the other whaling camps. This is a time of suspended action, as when the storyteller says of time long passed: *He did nothing…[long pause]…They did nothing…* A gap opens in the hurly-burly. On the margins of sleep or shamanistic soul-death, the characters hang in a void of non-action. Whether what they've done is praiseworthy or bad, the reflex generates inevitable response. Past events converge and we see what has happened. It is simply what it was. Everything is merely action. The specifics dissolve as we watch them recede into non-existence.

By now the sun is high and even in the wind it's warmer and ten of us dawdle round the tent, just waiting. The Three Muses sit smoking on the sled, creating a small, closed, female *qalgi*. Men arrive. Their snow-machines roar to the pressure-ridge behind us and they appear quietly on foot dragging their sleds. The younger men walk down to inspect the whale, talk among themselves and deferentially avoid Suluk. Suluk's contemporaries thrust their faces into his, gripping his shoulders, laughing with complicit happiness. Suluk softly talks logistics, carefully deflecting their pride in him to the fact of what he has to do. It all looks straight-forward. All we can see at its tether at the ice-edge is the dull black shine of the bowhead's torso like a huge slice of aubergine.

Earlier, Suluk stood by his whale with a couple of young crewmen, contemplating how to lift it from the water. He caught a whale two years ago, but he still lacks experience and needs the advice of an older man for both this and the butchering. He cannot afford to lose this whale or cut it up wrong. The village would lose tons of meat and he the equivalent in reputation. There are a number of older men, non-*umialiks*, to whom he can turn, and now he must make sure he gets one of them quickly. Men from other crews have arrived; they're waiting to start, and they want their shares. Latent in this quiet interlude, there's fever and urgency. The ice may shift and the whale go under. It must be butchered before its inner parts rot. Besides, we're expecting a final run of whales. Everyone wants to be back at their stations before the ice starts to break and forces them back to the village. Once the ice starts moving, the hunt will be over.

"Go get Tulugaq," Suluk murmurs, extrapolating his decision from his pain, where it had been shaping itself.

Before very long, and without anyone at first noticing, Tulugaq materializes. He is wearing a denim-covered sheepskin parka with a wolverine ruff and a blue woollen hat. A buck-knife hangs from a broad belt round his waist. Tulugaq, the Trickster I've known these two years in Max Lieb's nineteenth-century trading cabin, is transformed into a categorical and military figure, with disciplined step, decisive gestures and an authorative manner. Tulugaq has come to supervise. Cavities are chopped in the ice underfoot to form holding spars, and with block and tackle in place it takes fifty of us, fuelled with skin and blubber, a mere six hours to winch the whale up. And while Suluk hangs back in the wake of Tulugaq's authority, a day and night's labour of butchering begins.

Before long, like a goddess in a theatrical masque, Artemis makes her entry, transported in a quaint vehicle. The snow machine behind which she's travelling stops at the crest of the path through the pressure-ridge, and our female *umialik*, who has been sitting in the shelter of the basket-sled, descends cautiously. Artemis is wearing a parka-cover of shattering brilliance, its pattern of yellow, orange and green angles furiously interpenetrating against an electric blue ground. No Fauve could have designed an outfit more rebarbatively apt for a harpooner's spouse, nor one that could so out-shine the sea-ice. It is a dazzlingly sight: this meticulous woman, her parka-ruff high, stepping with self-consciously withheld excitement down to the water to inspect her latest, her own thirty-five tons, her personal behemoth.

As Artemis stands on the ice above the whale, her parka chiming hard on the snow and water, the whale's power cascades through her rigid body. The tension is terrific and her facial muscles, dancing behind a contemplative frown, to which her tinted glasses lend a dark, divine complexion, show its play. But Artemis must not reveal what triumph can do and she's superbly controlled. Rictus flickers just once at the corner of her mouth, and is straight away banished. Composure re-established, Artemis walks slowly to the tent to supervise the cooking. A cosmopolitan Inupiaq, as familiar with Alaskan town life as she is with the sea-ice, she's at the summit of what it is to be a Tikigaq woman. And when she emerges from the tent – that nineteenth-century Yankee whalers' innovation to provide women's quarters – she has regained her lovely, brawling, hard-edged multi-valency. It is right there in her language: controlling, complaining, accusing, logistically focused, yet always generous. "We have *yuukaq* (hot drink)," she cries sharp across the ice, the medial *k* and final *q* snapped off by her incisors, "But no *cups*!" – the syllable articulated as though to conjure, from the valley between consonants, what must be gathered. The Muses cringe as she stalks round camp, snapping mugs from the snow and returning to the tent with them bunched round her fingers.

We eat, and I notice that Artemis has brought not just breakfast, but also a new breakfast culture; and for the period that she is with us we dwell partly in this clock's sphere, that she has transported from the village. There is home-baked bread and a can of marmalade. The coffee, brewed in sea-ice water from an almost salt-free pressure ridge crest, suggests chicory or dandelion. It is a sublime and also a frightening breakfast, the coffee and marmalade lending a heraldic touch that parallels the black-and-white slices of whale skin we gild with mustard as it flops on our knives from the oily saucepan water. When I look up sleepily, I see Eli, our ten-year-old helper, perfecting the yoga of sliding (the *parama-sisu-asana*). "Cheap ice!" he murmurs when he loses his balance.

We start butchering the whale and almost all I know is the duration of labour, dragging meat and blubber on a long hook to the sleds where each share is trussed and carted to the village. Occasionally, someone hands me a pole-blade, and while he pulls with a hook, I work the knife through the blubber, which makes a shivering gradual crepitation, as though stitches in some thick, tight-sewn material are being torn from one another along the torso of a great diva. Sometimes the section I'm working on pulls away and whacks back in place over the meat, or else it peels off with a grinding, bloody slam and lands trembling across my boots.

The whale is dismembered with a kind of sagacious brutalism which Tulugaq supervises gravely. "Cut here, ah?" young men deferentially enquire. Tulugaq peers down his nose through dark glasses, as though absorbing information through his slightly pendulous lower lip, and breathes "*Ii*" in assent. Or he adjusts someone's knife along a line scored on the whale-skin, murmuring, "Cut here...to here..." Then he climbs back on the whale to study a new section. Suluk works alongside us. We talk quietly in English and Inupiaq. Then Tulugaq – as Raven – is deep within the carcass which has been opened for his descent, and conducts the operation from its centre, moving quietly with raised eyebrows and mouth half open among the viscera where the whale's souls dwelt. Sunk in this complex of ganglia – a vast, webbed, polychromatic rigging of filaments and glandular purple-and-white tissue – Tulugaq labours, brushing off the spent souls flocking to his snow-shirt and animating the whale's rib-cage till its body is half-empty and he emerges over the puddle of micro-fauna in its stomach contents which he himself spilled, flicking the blood from his glasses.

Except for the pounding of meat and blubber, and a definitive slap as the liver is extracted and the membrane peeled for an old man's drum-head, it's been peaceful in the body. And thus all the more perfect, as he straightens and finishes, is Tulugaq's long, concluding poly-morpheme: a musical line whose strange, inflected ending modulates, through a complicated flourish of laughter, back into silence where its impress shimmers. Work stops as the joke goes round the remains of whale and Tulugaq's *mot* is answered with an improvised counter-subject from a visiting *umialik*.

By now the senior personnel have sorted out their shares and sledded to the village to pave their caches in the permafrost with meat and *maktak*. Tulugaq, a widower, whose children live outside the village, is joined by his older brother, Sigvauna, a man of sixty, who has materialized as though by soul-flight from a southern village. Together, like shaman and assistant spirit, the brothers leave: Tulugaq kneeling nonchalantly with one leg bent on his worn-out skiddoo seat while Sigvauna, with a pirouette, jumps on one of the sled runners, and with one hand on the stanchion and one boot lifted, echoes Tulugaq's imbalance as though casually sealing with his own casual seniority his brother's authority. So they whistle off their meat, leaving us to plod round with the coarser ruck of Suluk's blubber.

Afterword

Gynaecology. They've not just operated on the whale, they are midwives to the sea. In this violently induced transaction, the murder of One, whose birth has been forced, is exchanged for the life-energy of many, the All joining everyone, so *their* births may continue.

When the whale's skull is rolled into the water, among the scarlet bubbles blasting to the surface, is the head-soul which the atlas vertebra had stoppered. Now this emerges through the skull's base and starts travelling south to be reborn in *agvigum nunanga* (the country of whales). Then another cry goes up, and the men shout "Come back when you're ready!" as though this whale's despatch already coincides with its re-birth as another.

– from: *Journal: May 23 1976*

Tom Lowenstein's books include *Ancient Land: Sacred Whale* (1993) and *Ancestors and Species* (2005).

ℬ

A Democratic Art:
Poetry In The Ukraine

OKSANA ZABUZHKO INTERVIEWED BY RUTH O'CALLAGHAN

Oksana Zabuzhko, awarded a PhD in Philosophy of Arts (1987), has held many fellowships and is Vice-President of Ukrainian PEN. Her publications include: five collections of poetry (one in English translation), literary studies and essays, translations, and the national bestseller *Field Work in Ukrainian Sex* (1996), which made her a major figure in contemporary Ukrainian literature, and has been translated into more than ten languages. She has received the Global Commitment Foundation Prize for Poetry, 1997, and several national awards.

ROC: In your letter of acceptance to the Global Commitment Foundation you mention that Ukrainian poetry is poorly known in the West. Could you outline some of the history?

OZ: Ukrainian literature has boasted a particularly strong tradition of poetry since the Baroque era (which, in the Ukraine, lasted from the sixteenth to the eighteenth centuries); and until the 1930s this tradition had never been interrupted, whatever turns the country's historical destiny took. Poetry, on the whole, is the most democratic of all arts: the least demanding in terms of the author's working conditions. Poems can be written on a walk, in a war trench, in a prison cell, and spread among readers hand-copied or by word of mouth. Poems by 'the Spinoza of the East', the great Ukrainian philosopher of the eighteenth century Hryhory Skovoroda, became part of our urban folklore long ago, and nowadays songs are still sung to his original tunes. Generally speaking, of all arts poetry is the least dependent on the social climate. This might explain the special place it occupies in endangered literatures, to which ours belonged for most of the nineteenth and twentieth centuries. In Tsarist Russia the Ukrainian language was officially banned, and it was due to the Western part of Ukraine, then incorporated into Austro-Hungary (where minority languages were allowed public usage), that Ukrainian literature was able to survive.

The 1920s are known in our history as the years of the 'Short Renaissance': it was then that modern Ukrainian literature reached its prime. It was also then that the first translations of Ukrainian poetry started to appear in the West: for example, works by Pavlo Tychyna, whose masterpiece *Instead of*

Sonnets and Octaves foretold the horrors of the twentieth century. Stalin's cultural purge in early-1930s Ukraine put an end to any cultural development for decades to come. In 1930-34, during the man-made famine (the notorious 'collectivization' now recognized as a genocide), the cultural elite of the country was exterminated. Some fifty thousand Ukrainian writers, artists and intellectuals fell victim to the purges; their works, along with most of the literary heritage of the past, were banned, and it wasn't until Khrushchev's brief 'thaw' that our literary fathers got a chance to start another Ukrainian Renaissance from scratch: trying to put right time which had gone out of joint, to restore the broken continuity of the literary tradition.

The liberation didn't last long. Brezhnev's 1970s brought another wave of purges upon the Ukrainian intelligentsia, even though these were minor in scale compared to the dark hole of Stalin's time. But I have vivid memories of the intoxicating atmosphere of the 1960s in which I grew up. I have the privilege of coming from a literary family – both my parents were professors of literature (later expelled from their jobs, among thousands of other Ukrainian intellectuals) – and our tiny apartment was always crowded with their enthusiastic students and colleagues, passionately discussing the country's past and present, rediscovering long-forgotten literary names, reading *samizdat*, and – most memorable for a child's ear – reciting poetry. Poets were then the cult figures of the generation. One of them, Vasyl Stus, who was later arrested – and died in a labour camp in 1985, when Gorbachev started to get rid of the political prisoners – has become a cultural icon. I think this was my emotional charge for a lifetime. Small wonder I started composing 'poems' before knowing how to put them down – since my sixth year – and have never stopped since.

Your generation of poets, the New Wave generation of the 1980s, wrote under entirely different circumstances to those of your parents. How did this come about, and how did you and your contemporaries keep Ukrainian poetic tradition alive?

We entered the literary scene as 'the children of liberty', driven, among other things, by a strong post-colonial impetus. Permeated, on the one hand, with sarcastic disgust for everything 'Soviet' – including a morally corrupt Soviet literary establishment which included neither gatekeepers nor role models for us – we were, at the same time, full of idealism, typical of cultural activists in all newly-liberating nations. We were eager to explore the spate of suddenly opened artistic possibilities, and determined to create a 'free literature for a free nation'. We started to read our poetry in public places, gathering hundreds of listeners. I remember reading at one of the political manifestations with which the Kiev of the late 1980s was swarming; and when, this summer [2008], I was invited to read at our most popular international ethno-rock festival *Kraina Mrij* – in the square, under an open sky, to a crowd of thousands – *déjà vu* evoked in me the revolutionary spirit of 20 years ago!

Did things change for poets with the fall of the Soviet Union and the Declaration of Ukrainian Independence in 1991? Did censorship paralyse or fuel poetry?

The German poet Hans Magnus Enzensberger once remarked (quite wittily, I daresay) that in any country, big or small, the number of true poetry lovers remains the same: about three thousand people. (Considering that my *Collected Poems* have sold six thousand copies in two years, I take his figure as accurate.) When I compare those crowds listening to poetry back in the late 1980s to nowadays, I see the difference in the quality of each audience. Those from pre-independence times were hungry for a 'free word', or simply a word in Ukrainian (which had been by then, even though not officially banned, marginalized, and pushed out of public usage), and were thus far more receptive to the political implication of a poem than its artistic power. On the other hand, you can be sure that present-day audiences are true poetry lovers.

And this is the major shift which I find most rewarding. I don't believe censorship does any good to poetry. What it can do, though, is to instil in poets a false sense of self-importance ("If they threaten me for my writing, then I must be important"), which, like any delusion, can be dangerous and, if it lasts long enough, may completely distort the poet's relationship with his or her talent, as well as that between poet and reader.

You refused to accept a nomination to Parliament, declaring it was "a writer's shortest route to degradation". Wouldn't this have been an opportunity to influence matters from within?

No, I don't think so. I believe writing and politics constitute two parallel circuits of power, which by definition should stay apart. To begin with, we use language differently. The writer's job is, to a large extent, similar to that of Biblical Adam – to name, for the first time, what's been previously unnamed – but no reasonable politician should ever say to the public what the public wouldn't already know. Another substantial difference lies in the fact that politicians are always interested in masses' feeling – and voting – alike, while authors are interested in individuals. Whenever authors switch to thinking in terms of mass feelings, they end up losing their original power to see people, and speak for them on the most personal level. It's like selling your birthright for nothing, for a mess of pottage.

How has Ukrainian poetry changed since the Orange Revolution?

Needless to say, political events of such a scale don't affect literature in an immediate way (unless it's bad literature!); but the whole of Ukrainian cultural life has become incomparably more vivid and animated since 2004. Within a year of the Orange Revolution, book sales all over the country had increased six-fold, and they continue to grow. Poetry has become marketable. People simply took a new interest in culture, and first and foremost this refers to the younger generation, to the so-called 'Children of Maidan' ('Maidan' is short for the Independence Square in Kiev where the 2004 uprising was centred). It's the Orange Revolution generation who call the tune. They wear T-shirts reading, "Time to read!", fight to protect historical sites and city parks from the unbridled lust of construction companies, hand-cuff themselves to entrance doors of bookstores under the threat of closure, and attend *en masse* the multiplying arts and literary festivals, poetry readings, literary cafes etc., to the great surprise of our Western colleagues, who are unaccustomed to see so many young people in the audience. In poetry, the past four years have brought an avalanche of new names. Ukrainian literature these days boasts probably one of the highest percentages of all European debuts.

Recently I took part in a round-table on Ukrainian-Russian literary connections, held by one of Russia's major literary magazines, and I was truly pleased to learn from my Russian colleagues that Ukrainian literature, and poetry in particular, is now winning popularity among Russian intellectuals as being "more interesting and dynamic" than their own. On Russian-language websites more and more poems of political resistance are appearing, most of them caustically satirical – an undeniable sign of life under a dictatorship.

To Western readers your website statement, "The writer's First Commandment should be Thou shalt not lie*", which you say makes the writer's job "a risky and dangerous one, similar to that of a diver or mountain climber" might appear exaggerated.*

I argue that telling the truth – bringing to the spotlight of people's consciousness what's been previously in shadow, whatever it may be – has been, and will always be, a risky job, for as long as human society exists: if only because, in pronouncing certain truths for the first time, you inevitably attack the whole set of psychological, mental, and verbal stereotypes which were disguising it. Virginia Woolf made a similar observation, in *Professions for Women*, when explaining her need to kill 'The Angel in the House'. Like any explorer, a writer sets out to undermine with their words the established order of things: and thus makes an easy target of himself, for people seldom like to be disturbed in their mental households.

To what extent does language define a sense of national identity?

In Soviet times, especially since the catastrophe of the 1930s, the struggle for the rights of the Ukrainian language had been close to the struggle for a national identity. Back in the 1970s and 1980s, people who dared to protest against imposed Russification were still sentenced in Ukraine to seven years of prison as Bourgeois Nationalists. Interestingly, nowadays, when Ukrainian is at last the official language of an independent state, many of those Ukrainians who grew up speaking Russian and with no access to Ukrainian schools recognize Ukrainian, according to the polls, as their "native language". Apparently, language still plays the role of an identity marker, of a symbolic citizenship to which they claim loyalty, even if they don't master it well.

However, dialogue conducted between writers of different nations, via international forums etc., does affect our "national cells" more than we imagine. I even believe that contemporary writers make up a kind of nation of their own. We all oppose the same adversary: the visual totalitarianism of mass culture, which stifles and mutes people's sensitivity.

Have Ukrainian women experienced any kind of a feminist movement, or did the struggle against political oppression obviate gender differences?

In Ukraine women's poetry has traditionally been strong, probably the strongest among the Slavs. We have classical cult figures, like Lesia Ukrainka (1871-1913) and Olena Teliha (1907-1942, shot by the Nazis in Babi Yar), who were glorified in the national pantheon as "more manly than men". It's due to the protective presence of these literary mothers that Ukrainian women's voices have never been easy to silence. Yet, as we all know, patriarchy can be quite inventive in its tricks, and knows how to impose its norms, even if in disguise. Soviet culture, with all its hypocritical discourse about 'women's liberation', managed to corral gender-articulate women's voices into a special women's ghetto, which I used to call 'The 8th of March Drawer', since it was on official Women's Day that love poetry by women filled the pages of the press, embellished by pictures of the authors *in their prime*. To make it in the mainstream, you were supposed to castrate yourself, to gender-neutralise your choice of subject as well as your language.

It wasn't until the 1990s that we could have a feminist revolution similar to the one you had in the 1970s. And I'm happy that I've made a contribution, as it was the scandal provoked in 1996 by the publication of my novel *Field Work in Ukrainian Sex* (which has a woman poet as its narrator) that finally opened the door from ghetto to mainstream for women writers. Similarly, my book *Notre Dame d'Ukraine* (2007) is the story of the silent war conducted for decades by patriarchal culture against one of the most interesting women literary heretics of the past century, our female classic, *Lesia Ukrainka* (1871-1913). The West is yet to discover her dramas: which, I'm sure will take their place among the highlights of European women's writing.

How has a Ph.D. in aesthetics influenced you as a writer?

I believe poetry and philosophy are quite compatible. Boris Pasternak graduated from a philosophy department, Ingeborg Bachman defended a thesis on Wittgenstein. And Nietsche was a poet, wasn't he? *Human, All Too Human* makes for wonderfully poetic reading! In Ukraine we have Hryhori Skovoroda, as I already mentioned. For me, poetry and philosophy are just two parallel ways to approach the mystery of being: in both, you address the world through moments when the dense fabric of everyday life tears, and speaking in Biblical terms, lets out "the hidden flame of being".

In 1994 you were a Fulbright Scholar, teaching Ukrainian literature at Harvard and the University of Pittsburgh. Did the 'Western dream' fulfil your expectations? Did you experience a culture shock?

In fact, *Field Work in Ukrainian Sex* was written during my stay in the US, and one of the key subjects of the book is precisely what critics in Eastern Europe have described as "the clash of an Eastern European intellectual with American culture". It's quite depressing to see how my premonitions concerning American civilization, as expressed in this novel, are coming true. When I first came to the US in 1992, as Writer in Residence at Penn State University, I was struck by innumerable similarities between two superpowers: the US, and the late USSR. On the other hand, I fell in love with red-neck America, with NYC and New England, with the profound democratic spirit, and unshakeable meritocratic instincts of the American people.

Do you find that literary criticism, the backbone of many university courses, frequently appears to have a set language in which to assess widely differing texts?

You've described very well what I call 'professorial blindness'. Of course, as an author, I might be biased; but my general feeling is that contemporary schooling is designed rather to kill a reader's empathy in prospective critics than to cultivate it. In my archive I keep a special file for 'irrelevant' reviews – those which, even when complimentary, left me open-mouthed – all of them written by university professors! It looks as if they were trained to pigeonhole a book in advance. Of course, there are exceptions, but usually I don't expect much of an understanding from this category of criticism. In a way, Octavio Paz was right when claiming that, to understand a poet, one has to be a poet oneself.

Are critics a necessary evil?

Critics are different. Sometimes they can be truly helpful, even inspiring – when they reveal to you something about your work that you didn't know yourself. And, yes, they are necessary: it's they who translate our writings into current public discourse, a mediation without which literature would have been sentenced to a hermetic existence in a cell of its own.

You have said that "translating the poets you admire opens you to new ways of feeling". Could you like to expand on this?

I believe that, for a poet, translating is as necessary as practising their instrument is for a musician. After all, language is our instrument, and it's hard to think of a more efficient way to keep it tuned than in translating those of your kin, who have played their tunes in other languages. It's like getting a blood transfusion: the original poem, which has struck you as somehow congenial to your own feelings, serves as an energy donor for a new poem which you re-create in your native tongue, thus overcoming its initial strangeness, having adjusted to your own breath and pulse. Admiration in this case stands for a form of kinship across linguistic barriers: poets, according to my experience, are usually able to recognize their brethren of the same 'blood group' in whatever linguistic disguise. Though I myself never dared to translate from languages that I don't know well enough, I admire Ingeborg Bachmann with her dense, convoluted, and, to my ear, incomprehensible German, no less than I do Sylvia Plath, or Marina Tsvetaeva, or Wislawa Szymborska, many of whose poems I know by heart in the original.

    I definitely prefer translations made by poets to those made by academics. Even in cases when the former don't fully master the language of the original, and indulges in poetic licence, there's always some chemistry between two poets which preserves at least some of the power of the original.

You have been called the Ukrainian Sylvia Plath. Was Plath an influence on you? Does your work also draw on familial relationships?

In my late 20s and early 30s I was very much under her spell. I was translating Plath's poetry like a madwoman, sucking from her a vitamin that I had been missing for my own work: the self-assuredness of a distinctly female voice. For, as our great playwright Lesia Ukrainka observed a century ago, women seldom have the confidence to say "it is". Rather, they choose to say "it seems to me": an observation not to be underestimated. I'm afraid that until now the "it-seems-to-me" way of thinking has preserved its power over many women writers, inhibiting their inner freedom. It was from Plath that I first learnt how literature can transmute female experience into a universal one – an invaluable lesson which helped me immensely in finding my own voice, both in poetry and in prose.

Familial relationships shape our personalities for life, and writing is, among other things, driven by authors' inexhaustible need to articulate conflicts conceived back in their childhood years. In a way, all writers are grown-up children: children who have learnt to speak for themselves. And I'm no exception in this regard. As a fiction writer, I'm quite obsessed with family stories, not in the least because it's from them that the real texture of every national history is woven, which doesn't necessarily coincide with the official national narrative.

What is the poet's place in society? Does it differ from the novelist's?

It certainly does. Poets are and will always remain the guardians of a language, which every society tries to contaminate with lies of its own. Unlike novelists, who may be pigeonholed as opinion-makers, poets are seldom interviewed by media on political and moral issues, yet in the end it's they who remain responsible for the very human capacity to opine. They keep our language alive.

Ruth O'Callaghan's latest collection *A Lope Of Time* (Shoestring) was published in 2009.

℘

Evan Jones
For Peter Porter On His Eightieth Birthday

Old doppelgänger, as always
you precede me. With the same limping gait
I follow you up stairs, as ever
two-and-a-half steps behind.
Wait for me at the top, wherever that is.

REVIEWS
&
ENDPAPERS

℘

Considering poems by people who have not yet published
a book is an excellent way of sampling how poets estimate
stylistics at a particular time of crisis
– *Peter Porter*

Themes And Variations

STEVEN MATTHEWS

Ciaran Carson, *Collected Poems*, Gallery Books, €25, ISBN 978185235432

To read straight through this handsomely-produced *Collected* is to be reminded of the strongly-determining core narrative that drives Carson's work from book to book. What can sometimes seem frustratingly cryptic or enigmatic as each new volume appears is often clarified by referring back to earlier poems. There is a dialogue backwards and forwards within the work, which makes it a unique, if sometimes self-intent, closed circuit. In other words, there is a mighty verve pushing forward the whole project, a verve which coins the often eruptive energies at the level of the individual poem. The whole career reads as a set of variations upon an early-established understanding about the precariousness of the world out of which, and about which, Carson writes.

These backwards and forwards energies even operate at the level of the image. For instance, the concatenation of love with time in the last book, *For All We Know*, which is developed through a set of images involving wristwatches, recalls 'Two the Tango' from *First Language* (1993):

> She watched the way the hair on his wrist curled round
> the band of his wrist-watch.
> This is an example of 'initial entanglement', from which
> it's difficult to wrench
>
> Herself.

Such lines remind us that, for all the jazzy colloquialism of the extended lines that have characterised Carson's poetry from the mid-1980s, there is a brilliant technique at work. The line endings dramatically mirror what is being described, the rhymes provide a skeletal and barely-noticed structure upon which the energetic voice is hung. Moving "round" enclosed worlds, whilst bearing the "wrench" of what threatens to tear them apart, is the experience which Carson has always written about, and forms the experience of reading his work. Clues laid in the earlier work often burgeon into full expositions in the later. The street names in Belfast derived from Napoleonic or Crimean battles provided something of the disorientation, as well as reminders of continuing military colonisation, in *The Irish For No* (1987) and *Belfast Confetti* (1989). By *Breaking News* (2003), we have a whole sequence, 'The War Correspondent'. As a key poem, 'Jawbox', has it, "It's that effect where one image warps into the other".

What determines that warping, ultimately, is the experience of living in Belfast at the time of the Troubles, and Carson is surely the most enduring, as well as critically-shrewd, chronicler of that experience. This is the Belfast of sudden explosions, of familiar landmarks suddenly obliterated from the map. It is a place constantly being watched and scrutinised by the British forces; of coded messages being passed in secret by one side or the other. Carson's poetry absorbed all of that and more, particularly attuned to do so, he suggests, because of his family background amongst those whose first language is Irish. At moments, Carson casts himself as poet professionally following in the footsteps of his postman father, as 'Second Language', about the learning of English, sees it:

> I love the as-yet morning, when no-one's abroad, and I am like
> > a postman on his walk,
> Distributing strange messages and bills, and arbitrations with
> > the world of talk […]

'Abroad', the colloquialism, furnishes also a nice pun, reminder of the alienated nature of this situation, but also of the opportunity which it provides, since "the future looms into the mouth incessantly, gulped-at and unspoken". Of course, the conveyer of these "strange messages" is not necessarily better placed than anyone else to know what they mean. But "What comes next is next […] an angel whispers of the here and now". In the meantime, Carson's collections of the 1980s provide a series of frequently hilarious snapshots and narratives of the scene on the ground, since, as 'Belfast Confetti' has it, "I know this labyrinth so well".

As that scene has mercifully become quieter, Carson, like all Irish writers, has adapted his poetry to the new situation. Primarily a writer who from the start saw language and voicing as central to the issue, he has been better-placed and more successful than most in doing so. The bizarreness of Margaret Thatcher's command that Sinn Féin should not be heard, brilliantly relished in several poems ("We cannot reproduce his actual words here […] An actor spoke for him"), reminds us of the licence Carson has always taken within and between voices and languages, as reflected in the enigmatic and moving Euro-zone romantic relationship of *For All We Know*. True, there have been wrong turnings along the way. The hallucinatory, drunkenly-warped worlds of *Opera Et Cetera* and *The Twelfth of Never*, whatever their inventiveness, are over-blown and will test the patience of readers, however much they seek to claim authority from Coleridge and De Quincy. The William Carlos Williams-inspired brief poems in *Breaking News* underwhelm. But, all in all, the self-reference of Carson's poetic works to good effect, carried as it is by the clever energies of his style. This is a unique and urgent *Collected* which demands revisiting across its course.

Steven Matthews is a writer and teacher who lives in Oxford.

ᘓ

The Raven In Ravening

DAVID MORLEY

John F. Deane, *A Little Book of Hours*, Carcanet, £9.95, ISBN 9781857549706; Martin Harrison, *Wild Bees: New and Selected Poems*, Shearsman Books, £7.95, ISBN 9781848610088

In an anguished polemic titled 'Dream of a Fair Field', published in *The Furrow*, the fine Irish poet and editor John F. Deane wrote,

> The ground of all my living and writing has been an attempt to fashion a language and imagery suitable to the translation of Christian faith in these modern times, and for this I have suffered ridicule and rejection [...] How can [a poem] bring a sense of integrity and morality to a political system in our own country that works by subterfuge, aiming at perpetuation of power rather than the good of the citizens when political life has become shameful and overtly dismissive of the deeper values by which Christianity ought to flourish? A poet may be noisily praised and lauded in public but is ignored and dismissed as having nothing 'real' to offer to the 'real' world.

I quote from this essay because the poet intends it to be read and considered: the piece is republished on Deane's personal website. If we accept that these are legitimate assertions and questions for a poet of faith, then Deane's beleaguered response is perfectly understandable. However, the stance of his language gives the impression that Christian faith is already cornered – by the "'real' world", even though Deane is sharing that corner with his God. Poetry gets him (and his faith) out of this corner. Poetry serves his cause (and his God) clearly and beautifully.

The poems in *A Little Book of Hours* release little worlds; Deane's perplexity becomes articulate energy and the means for clear-eyed self-exploration, exploring if not quite never answering those questions from his essay. Here is an indicative passage from the poem 'Towards a Conversion'. In Deane's poems an ecological sense of conversion, of 'translation', is always tangible within his spiritual perceptions:

> [...] I walk over millennia, the Irish
> wolf and bear, the elk and other
> miracles; everywhere bog-oak roots
>
> and ling, forever in their gentle
> torsion, with all this floor a living thing, held
> in the world's care, indifferent. Over everything
> voraciously, the crow, a monkish body hooded
>
> in grey, crawks its blacksod, cleansing music;
> lay your flesh down here you will become
> carrion-compost, sustenance for the ravening roots;
> where God is, has been and will ever be.

I admire the spoken music here: the mind's flight-path for the crow across lines and stanza; and the transformational release of the raven in "ravening". Good news for his readers that all the poems in the book are as wide-awake and as interesting as this example. The long elegy 'Madonna and Child' is the masterwork, eventfully spiritual, almost a dream-work in the way it stirs at memory – which is both observed and imagined. In 'Dream of a Fair Field' the poet mourned the loss to contemporary poetry of the language of the 'Song of Solomon'. In 'Madonna and Child' he liberates and refreshes this same language for his own invocations and revivifications:

> As an orchid among buttercups is she, as a peach tree
> among brambles in the wood; as exile
> in a hostile land, as drudge among the very poor.

Michael Symmons Roberts wrote in a recent *Poetry Review*, "The relationship between creative freedom and religious belief is far from limiting [...] religious faith was an imaginative liberation [...]" That's true of John F. Deane when he is creating poems. However, in the same way that the composer John Tavener's work has been seen as more of a challenge to the world than a consolation, Deane's writing offers: "the rising recurrent sorrow of the merely human before loss, its unacceptability, its disdain" ('Madonna and Child'). These are beautiful, solemn, gravid poems, best read aloud for, like John Tavener, Deane has to be heard to be believed.

Joy in making, seeing and connecting; simplicity without simplification; complexity without complication: that's a single-breath summary of Martin Harrison's hugely impressive poetic technique, a technique I feel caught out by in all the nicest ways. His work was entirely new to me yet I felt immediately at home in these fresh, vivid poems. I'm sure most British readers will feel the same, especially if they are familiar with the techniques of Robert Frost, Les Murray, Elizabeth Bishop, Raymond Carver and Allen Curnow. Yes, those influences are there but Martin Harrison is very much his own maker: he's simply assimilated the best of these poets as he travelled through their diction.

Harrison has travelled the world; his early years were in England. There's a fine and painful poem about his father, a travelling wine salesman and amateur poet in Northern England who in the evenings "jotted screeds of 'nature poetry'":

> He called it doing the accounts.
> Sincerely, he hoped I'd do more, with more success:
>
> but "*study money, not poetry*" was his long-lived, bleak
> advice. In his 80s now, his steady observation:
> "*I've given up making sense of things. Work only*
>
> *for yourself.*" A palimpsest is what's scraped away:
> a scarping which reveals a trace, a 'beneath' that's covered
> over with new scrawl. Are memories like that trace?
> ('Letter from America')

Harrison spent some time in New Zealand before settling in Australia. He's an exported – now imported – writer of unusual range and observational skill, and that sense of being outside things helps him write some of the most brilliant metaphyical nature poems of our time, for example in 'The Platypus':

[...] it can shift from one medium
to another—from scrabble to dig to swim.
Fur, blood and bones, it lives out a warm theorem:
how cells communicate with mode and shape.
It's pure exuberance of style. No post-modern,
it benefits from natural history. No victim,

it even shows how to adjust thoughts to
that maya, that dream, where illusion's both true
and false [...]

In poems like 'The Platypus', 'The Coolamon', 'Stopping for a Walk in Reserved Land Near Murra Murra', 'Late Western Thought' and the two 'Letters from America', Martin Harrison takes a natural setting or creature and explores it scrupulously, writing it sideways – or should I say he allows the pressures of the developing poem to write him sidelong: images blinking in at themselves, birdlike in their movement through his mind's eye and the mind of the reader.

Sometimes the process risks sentimentality, but that's one of the recognised hazards when writing such technically brilliant and emotionally alive poems, and Harrison gets it right each time. I recommend *Wild Bees* with extreme prejudice; this book altered my mood, my whole day and made me write a new poem.

David Morley's next collection is forthcoming from Carcanet Press in 2010.

Squeezed And Bubbling

SARAH CROWN

Medbh McGuckian, *My Love Has Fared Inland*, Gallery Press, £9.95
ISBN 9781852354527;
Josephine Dickinson, *Night Journey*, Flambard, £7.50
ISBN 9781906601010

"It was a bright inviting, freely formed," says Medbh McGuckian in the opening breath of her opening poem, 'Painting by Moonlight',

> though I suppose it was I who brightened,
> with an internal scattering of light [...]

On first reading, the glancing light, quick skitter of consonants and self-effacing "I suppose" conspire to deny our eyes purchase on these lines, sending us sliding past before we can consider them too closely. Turn back to the first page after finishing the collection, however, and they seem to hover over the book like an epithet: perfectly describing the "bright inviting" of McGuckian's chiaroscuro lines; the "freely formed" wheel and dive of poems that call to mind the unfettered late modernism of JH Prynne; the poet's own position as hub and focus of her poetic universe. McGuckian has summed up her whole enterprise in a handful of words – then placed them in such a way that we seem almost bound to overlook them.

But such deflection is characteristic, too. As a reader of McGuckian's work one feels, if not voyeuristic, certainly incidental. She herself is the one fixed point in this collection: time, landscape and language spin and collide around her in poems so fiercely inward-looking that they scarcely seem to require an audience. Sometimes dizzying, often baffling (with surfaces gorgeous but lacquered, like oil paintings, forbidding penetration), what her poems do afford is the rare experience of seeing the world as it truly appears when filtered through someone else's perception.

And what a world McGuckian looks out on. Colour drenches it, as both subject and tool, deepening and enriching descriptions ("Slight colour from the weak, late-night sunlight, / lesser reds, like a barely broken dawn") or used synaesthetically to characterise a mood: "black anxiety"; "cinnamon demureness"; "a gentle pink, close to pain". Landscapes and bodies are her terrain; she pores over them with equal intensity, their essential instability resolved in the moments they unite, as when a man "looking out of second-storey / windows at our fields" remembers "landscapes sedimented" in his lover's body; "silk-tongued rains / that stormed her island by island". The weather works its way through the seasons, too, which McGuckian uses frequently as anchors to her imaginings ("It was a fragrant December. Satin-voiced."). Predictably, however, in McGuckian's universe such anchors drag: as we read on, her seasons shift like tectonic plates, sliding over, buckling under, joining and dividing until we find ourselves dazzled by "an April setting in the winter of words", "summer-lidded mountains, clearing autumn skies".

The images are strikingly lovely, but make no mistake: this is challenging poetry. In her pursuit of truth, McGuckian works at language's outer edges, employing a personal iconography so complex that it must be accepted rather than fully grasped; felt, rather than understood. Go with it, though, and this collection has the power to amaze the senses, blurring the boundaries between words, pictures and music.

While there's a linguistic exuberance to Josephine Dickinson's work that lends it a superficial similarity to McGuckian's (listen to her voluptuous description of a ship at night: "The boat stinks of tar and purrs like a bull [...] At prow and helm lit torches dribble"), the similarity ends there. Where everything is on the move in McGuckian's universe, the fundamentals of Dickinson's cosmos are more durable. She is concerned, rather, with the manner in which objects move through the stillness – from rivers, "flowing silver", "squeezed / and ... bubbling", to light, to the planets themselves, which veer from physical into metaphysical, science (Venus "is 108 million kilometres from the Sun and has a 243-day rotation period") into myth ("don't sing to me of Jupiter, or Saturn, / or a coiled up golden fleece").

This voyage through the solar system is just one of the "night journeys" which Dickinson paints for us. Fast on its heels comes a far more intimate sequence, 'This Night', in which darkness itself is rendered fitfully, subtly visible ("Dense trees / joust in the shadows // carry dark rooms, / develop likenesses"), and which describes, among other things, the speaker's own fumbling progress through a night of Stygian gloom ("I clutched at twigs [...] By feet and skin, / by the stump / of a broken chestnut tree / we found the fifth bridge [...]"). It's impossible to ignore the metaphorical weight of such a journey; sure enough, in the next sequence, 'Elegies' (written for the poet's late husband, Douglas) the metaphor moves decisively from subtext into text. Through agonizingly restrained descriptions of her husband's decline, she gives us two different night-journeys: his transition from life into death, and her parallel passage through a period of spiritual darkness; a journey into night, and a journey through it.

And yet, despite the subject matter, it's at this moment that Dickinson's poetry begins to shoulder free of the shadows. The poems are set about with bright objects – a glass of water, "cold and clear", plums that "glowed orange" – while dark is lit up with "phosphorescent grass", stars that "sizzle in the water", until the speaker confesses that she "no longer see[s] the night". Although darkness returns in the final poems, it is softer, warmer; reminding us what else the night is for. Dickinson concludes her collection with a series of love poems as blissful and celebratory as any I've read. "Your body ripples inside / me" she says in the final lines of her penultimate poem, 'In the Darkness',

> and the filaments of your face take
> shape and glow in that invisible space
> and dizzyingly fill the space with light.

Night and journey are both over: a new day has dawned.

Sarah Crown is the *Guardian*'s Online Literary Editor.

ℬ

Life In Art

KIT FAN

Clive James, *Angels Over Elsinore: Collected Verse 2003-2008*,
Picador, £14.99, ISBN 9780330457408;
John Kinsella, *Comus: A Dialogic Mask*, Arc, £12.99, ISBN 9781906570231

The titles of these new books by Australian poets call up the ghosts of Shakespeare and Milton. Though both are literary and revisionary poets, neither conforms to the notion of the Empire writing back.

Clive James is one of the most prolific and high-profile Australian writers of today, but not usually thought of as a poet. In 'Portrait of Man Writing', near the end of this riveting collection, the poet describes a painter "lending inwardness to an outline" to "record the damage" of the sitter's years. Underneath the poem's flirtatious surface concern with age differences is a moving meditation on 'life in art': "Suppose while you paint me I wrote of you / with the same fidelity". The poem raises troubling questions about "integrity", "truth", and "fidelity", concluding offhandedly that "your portrait, [...] put in words, sounds like a lie". What is implicated is not only whether painting and poetry are comparable on those terms, but the subtle, elegiac undertone of time past ("the mortal clockwork" that ticks "towards the day we fall apart"), revealing a "real life" beyond the many masks and guises in James's earlier satire *Peregrine Prykke's Pilgrimage*.

An inquisitive and restless sitter, James is a real portrait painter: of the dreamy, sensuous woman with "Monica Bellucci skin" in 'Woman Resting', the unlikely literary couple in 'Publisher's Party', the "riddled corpse" of the member of Hamas in 'Yusra', and a lonesome immigrant working at a kiosk in 'Naomi from Namibia'. Stripped off their high gloss of rhyme and playfulness, these portraits show a sense of casual attentiveness to subject and object, as where the speaker in the 'Museum of the Unmoving Image' records and questions "a glass case" or "a shrivelled pea", remembering a "speech" that was "vivid with specific things". Specific things, like people, matter to James. The best example is 'When We Were Kids', a breathtaking poem that shimmers with childhood memorabilia – Shelley's lemonade, a Scout belt buckle, and Thundercracker: the obscure objects of previous desire poignantly resurrected.

Though the book shows a dazzling range of forms, subjects, and voices, it gravitates towards two heartbreaking elegies ('My Father Before Me' and 'At Ian Hamilton's Funeral') and two exceptional poems of homage ('Belated Homage to Derek Walcott' and 'Les Saw It First'). Travelling between continents, family history and literary friendship, these four poems share a tonal equanimity – a resolute openness towards death and sorrow, and on lifelong efforts of affection towards his literary friends. At the end of his elegy for Hamilton, James speaks of "the awareness of love, how it defends / Itself against forgetfulness". James's best poems, armoured with tight rhymes, share this heightened awareness of love and loss.

The book remembers many real places where the heart breaks: San Wan War Cemetery in Hong Kong, the Public Morals Unit of Hamas, the Yasukuni Shrine, and James's Australia (Sydney, the creek at Inverell, and Brisbane Botanical Gardens). However, it also evokes Hamlet's Elsinore as its central poetic premise. In the title poem, James takes us through "the ideal world", a plot driven by the Christian afterlife, before exorcising us to back to the stage where "some clown" picks up "his skull" and utters the dramatic line "Alas". Like 'Portrait of Man Writing', the title poem explores the paradox of life in art. *Angels Over Elsinore* begins with the linguistic playfulness of 'Windows Is Shutting Down' and ends with the elegiac 'We Being Ghosts'. Its breadth, diversity, and formal ease confirm James as a fascinating poet as well as an antic performer of other genres.

Decoding Milton's chastening masque about chastity into an exhilarating "environmental dialogic poem" of the twenty-first century, John Kinsella recasts Comus as an "out of control" genetic scientist, an "unethical bio-engineer" addicted to Viagra and committed to "years of research and pleasure", knowing "the gene that awakes / fields of rape". Comus's counterpoint and snare, "the Lady", becomes an eco-warrior who pities his "artificial magic" and "self-asserting rhetoric", sharply pinpointing that something is rotten in the state of science – "the new sublime of waste / and desecration" that teeters "on the edge / of holocaust". The effect is a powerful rendering of Milton's sexually perverse *Comus* into a moving ecological play that evokes the pastoral beauty of English and Australian landscape ("the green vine that winds its way / along the small hill on the wood's edge") and the atrocity of the synthetic sublime (the "cycle of plasma greenery, worship / of cars and technology"). As Kinsella succinctly puts it in the Afterword: "the basic sexual hypocrisy is also the hypocrisy of the abuse of the land".

Despite Kinsella's "direct approach of Milton's cybernatic / folktale", the question at the heart of the play is much more challenging than it first seems: when "war" strikes "at the heart of forests", how, on the "'perplexing / path of 'sustainability'", can we find a way for "a science / that co-exists with forests"? The answer, if any, might be found in Sabrina's song, which Tim Cribb identifies in his brilliant introduction as a "bond" and continuity between the masques by Milton "the republican regicide" and Kinsella "the vegan anarchist". Two Sabrinas synchronise to invoke an antediluvian world of beasts and changing landscape. Whilst Milton's Sabrina sings to "save", Kinsella's wishes to "recover", a beautifully tuned word that signals change and recuperation.

Kit Fan completed his PhD on Thom Gunn at the University of York. He is currently working on his first collection of poems.

❧

Satire And Sensibility

JANE HOLLAND

Wendy Cope, *Two Cures for Love: Selected Poems 1979-2006*, Faber, £12.99,
ISBN 9780571237395; Maureen Duffy, *Family Values*, Enitharmon, £8.95,
ISBN 9781904634607; Patience Agbabi, *Bloodshot Monochrome*,
Canongate, £8.99, ISBN 9781847671530

Wendy Cope is the wittiest poet writing in Britain today. That's the conclusion I came to on reading her *Selected Poems*: laughing so hard that I cried, so loud that my husband came in to complain. But I couldn't help it. Her light, satirical touch is devastating, even when turned on herself in 'Making Cocoa for Kingsley Amis': "I knew it wouldn't be much of a poem / But I love the title."

This *Selected* has Notes and an illuminating Preface. I thoroughly approve of notes in poetry collections, poets being an obscure bunch in general; without these, I might have been stumped by some of the more satirical pieces, particularly those aimed at fellow poets. But many of her poems need no explanation at all, with their laser-eyed observation of society's more absurd foibles. The one about the School Inspector and the "dead stickleback", for instance, hurt my sides. 'Reading Scheme', based on those tediously repetitive 1970s Ladybird books, is equally funny. Here, Daddy comes home early, catching Mummy with the milkman: "Daddy looks very cross. Has he a gun? / Up milkman! Up milkman! Over the wall!"

Brilliant on men, Wendy Cope is particularly merciless when it comes to male poets. Here you will find hilarious imitations of Larkin, Hughes, Heaney, Hill – "'Pack it in,' said Duffa, 'and buy me a drink.'" – and Raine, all written in the persona of Jason Strugnell, amateur poet extraordinaire. And her 'Waste Land Limericks', a rewrite of T.S. Eliot's classic poem – "Met Stetson and gave him an earful" – with one limerick per section, ought to be required reading on English syllabuses everywhere:

> The Thames runs, bones rattle, rats creep;
> Tiresias fancies a peep –
> A typist is laid,
> A record is played –
> Wei la la. After this it gets deep.

There are serious moments too, with a poem here for those who died in the 9/11 attacks, but Cope's real forté as a poet is satire from a female perspective. One of her most famous pieces, 'My Lover', is an examination of the male psyche instantly recognisable to all women: "For I will consider my lover, who shall remain nameless. / For at the age of 49 he can make the noise of five different kinds of lorry changing gear on a hill." And if you needed any further persuasion, I shall close with her superb four-liner 'Timekeeping':

> Late home for supper,
> He mustn't seem drunk.
> 'The pob cluck,' he begins,
> And knows he is sunk.

Maureen Duffy also delights in addressing other practitioners of her craft. *Family Values* is the somewhat mundane title of this selection of poems written since 1989. Duffy is an unvarnished writer; she addresses issues head-on and in plain language, never straining for a poetic effect but perfectly at home in the medium, breathing it naturally. A poet's poet, one might say.

In 'Voices', Duffy describes the "hallucinatory power" of the past as something dangerous, to be avoided. Not surprisingly, however, her poems still dwell on "half glimpsed mist-wraiths", with moving elegies "for the lately dead who / barely lived." 'Lament for the Scribblers' wonders with a beautiful and melodious economy why old poets aren't better at surviving hard winters, and why some manage to keep writing until they "drop / like the tarry stares that feathered the telegraph wires / in October" while others struggle to keep up with them, "our pockets crackling with obsequies to bribe / wisdom out of your lines and lives".

Duffy's poems are often loose on punctuation, allowing lines to slam into each other, words to tumble headlong over meaning, sometimes precipitous, sometimes slowing to pinpoint significance. Yet they are always musical and unerringly aware of their direction, like the whistling blind man in the opening poem, 'Blues Underground', whose "stick taps out a pattering rhythm" as his tune exhorts commuters to praise every morning.

One of the themes behind her work is the contrast between town and country living, or rather, the ability to live rurally even in the heart of suburbia. Birds feature strongly, nesting or giving off "avian shrieks", and green shoots are everywhere, suggestive of rebirth and continuing growth. Duffy links poetry with such natural activities, as others have done before her – "The blackbirds are building again / my Spring monitors, urban cousins / of Clare's thrushy minstrels" – and so fits herself snugly into a long and venerable tradition.

Rather less snug is Patience Agbabi in *Bloodshot Monochrome*, her third poetry collection, though clearly looking to inhabit similar territory with fourteen prose 'sonnets' based around famous poets, a sort of 'guess the writer' sequence entitled 'Problem Pages'. For instance, 'Send My Roots Rain' is based on the sublime sonnet by Gerard Manley Hopkins which, like Duffy's poem above, compares nest-building to the act of writing poetry. Here, it is transformed into: "Dear Patience, I'm a priest first and a poet / second. I seek inspiration not publication." In the concluding sestet, Patience replies prosaically: "Confront your conflict of interests. You may be a / poet second but your writing should always come / first."

Nostalgia is thick elsewhere in this collection, with poems recalling both real and imagined pasts in her 'Shots' and 'Monologues' sections. Most are intended for performance rather than the page, which makes them difficult to assess fairly. Many seem genuinely felt, and some of the shorter poems here, moving towards lyric, are successful: "I bit the Big Apple. Black, impatient, young. / A string of pips exploding on my tongue." This more sensuous note is welcome, and collides happily with Agbabi's off-beat humour: "My heart was break // dancing on the road to Wigan Casino, / Northern Soul Mecca where transatlantic bass / beat blacker than blue in glittering mono."

Overall though, Agbabi's range is limited and her work uneven: "You can't find a good gay shag unless you pay for it" begins an expletive-rich poem about internet dating. Her poem, 'Eat Me', about female obesity, errs on the side of offensive; after she has suffocated her partner with her body, the "beached whale" narrator closes with: "There was nothing else left in the house to eat." Satire, yes, but perhaps not in the best possible taste.

Jane Holland is the editor of *Horizon Review*; her latest collection is *Camper Van Blues* (Salt).

Voice Registration

ALEX SMITH

Pauline Stainer, *Crossing the Snowline*, Bloodaxe, £8.95, ISBN 9781852248123;
Mary Oliver, *Red Bird*, Bloodaxe, £8.95, ISBN 9781852248116

One of the first things to claim a reader's attention is the registration of a poet's voice, the tone in which the images, narrative, rhetoric and so on are couched. And this registration is often the key to the poem's marriage of form and content. In the two volumes of lyrical poems under consideration, the registration the poets adopt could not be more different.

The work of Pauline Stainer is so extraordinary that it is difficult to convey its power adequately. *Crossing the Snowline* is her first collection since *The Lady & the Hare: New & Selected Poems* (Bloodaxe, 2003), and it again displays her startling use of imagery – which can be unsettling, even stark. There is never an easy consolation. Familiar with medieval culture, Stainer often employs Christian symbolism obliquely, in ways that are both contemporary and highly original. Her Christ, when he occasionally appears, permeates nature with his wounds, and it is this deep sympathy with suffering humanity that gives her work its raw power.

The poems tend to breathe within a slight frame, sparse and short lined, with most – in this volume, all – fitting onto a single page. 'The Flaying of Marsyas (after Titian)' is just four stanzas long. Here are the last two:

> Ecstasy
> strips to the quick:
> the suspended satyr
> sheds his senses
> with eyes wide-open.
>
> Cool inspiriting,
> when poets hear
> the cuckoo call
> as soldiers die
> in one another's arms.

Stainer is a master of ekphrasis but all her poems are intensely visual; they are nothing if not eidetic.

A perceived continuum of phenomena across time and space informs Stainer's work. Events of significance, springing from however humble a source, extend across both history and geography. Here are the opening stanzas of the title poem, 'Crossing the Snowline':

> I still see them –
> the sculptors of Kilpeck
> on the road
> to Santiago de Compostela,
> crossing the Roman bridge
> in the small hours
>
> westward,

always westward,
Finisterre referring
its azure,
the jubilation of wolves
spilling into the cloister.

Each line and word is carved with such precision that images often have the force of myth – e.g., "the jubilation of wolves" (presumably taken from Durwood L Allen). Time and again the reader goes back over this volume to re-engage with these remarkable poems. But the tone of the work is deceptively low key: the poet herself usually nowhere in sight. There are times, for this reader at least, when it's as if we're exploring a territory similar to that of Celan, or the Geoffrey Hill of *For the Unfallen* (although without the former's hermetic difficulty or backdrop of terror). This might seem a high claim to make, but Stainer's work belongs in this company.

Beyond the symbols of glass, water, lenses, hares and – above all – light, are the occasional figures of Christ and Mary, rendered mysterious as though we're learning of them afresh. Nothing in Stainer's work could be further from the didactic or the overtly pious. The poems are simply allowed to speak for themselves. For the reader unfamiliar with her work, *Crossing the Snowline* is a good place to start.

Mary Oliver, however, is a presiding presence throughout her latest volume, *Red Bird*. A popular poet in the United States, she is very much at the centre of her poems, and always has a story to tell. We are invited to share, and empathise with, her state of feeling, whether about the natural world – she lived for many years on Cape Cod – or in her "first-ever cycle of love poems", as the book cover has it:

I wish I loved no one,
I said, one long day [...]

Many of these poems are well-enough crafted and move with purposeful momentum toward their conclusion, but the reader is subjected to the insistently didactic tone of the poet's voice throughout: often with a reverential, breathless quiet following a natural piety. The book cover says that Oliver extends "the visionary American tradition of Whitman, Emerson, Frost and Emily Dickinson". This is nonsense; nothing could be more remote from Dickinson. But one can clearly understand why Oliver is a popular poet; the poems, persuasive, therapeutic even, would fit in well over here with Thought for the Day.

Part of the problem concerns redundancies, with the poet simply getting

carried away with her own language. The volume opens with the title poem,
'Red Bird':

> Red bird came all winter
> firing up the landscape [...]

which is a strong image, arresting the reader at the start. So far, so acceptable;
but the third line (the poem is in three-line stanzas) is "as nothing else could",
which weakens their impact. It doesn't help that these lines are virtually
repeated at the end of the poem – after the poet has told us that she is "a God-
fearing feeder of birds".

Having said this, I am sure that the poems in this book will satisfy a good
number of readers: although they might not all be readers of *Poetry Review*.

Alex Smith last volume of poems was *Ocean Myths* (Ino Press, 1999).

℘

Visionary Stocktaking

DOUGLAS HOUSTON

Peter Porter, *Better Than God*, Picador, £8.99, ISBN 9780330460675

Better Than God unflaggingly sustains the momentum of Peter Porter's
work through his seventeen major collections to date. The book adds
new dimensions of creative reach and technical excellence to an oeuvre
distinguished by imaginative audacity and mastery of a wide range of poetic
forms. There are poems here that continue to surprise with Porter's gift for
strikingly unexpected conceptions. 'In Bed with Oblomov', for example, is a
dramatic monologue in the voice of Sleep, whose lulling cadences persuasively
incite Goncharov's sloth-bound hero to surrender to oblivion: "[...] but be
with me / At drowsing's edge and share the dust / Which lullabies the noise
of coach and street. / Pull blankets up, give it your trust, / This love bed made
for just one pair of feet."

While art – literary, painterly, and musical – has consistently informed
Porter's poetry, science and technology have also been points of reference in
charting his remarkably expansive thematic territory. The attempts at the
CERN laboratory to recreate the universe's beginnings are the focus of 'The

Apprentice's Sorcerer', the human compulsion for the getting and growth of knowledge culminating in a project with apocalyptic implications: "Perhaps in this Swiss hole the world will see / A proof beyond its statutory Big Bang / And hear that what the Morning Angels sang / Was more then some wide-screened banality." That last line rings with the disaffection from our cultural status quo that has long fuelled Porter's incisive critiques of how we live in the spirit of Auden's injunction to artists that "Whoever rules, our duty to the City / is loyal opposition" ('The Garrison'). The prescriptive dumbing-down of life and art is dismissed with the hammer-and-tongs light verse of 'To Murder Sleep': "The world is forcing us to show / That relevance may not go slow, / That what might fit is not allowed, / That 'Art To Go' will please the crowd / While self-elected prophets dwell / In Academia's arc-en-ciel."

Porter's engagement with the human condition goes, however, far beyond anything resembling satire in a number of the most striking poems in the book. The doubleness of selfhood and consciousness – "The Questioner who sits so sly / Is I one moment then it's Me" in 'Moi à Égard du Je' – is a reiterated theme that links with that of cognition as exile from the fundamental nature of reality, most notably in 'Lost Among the Lizards': "[...] I cannot feel / That warm-limbed lizard-like phenomenon / Of living in the real world, the real / Unpersuaded territory where / No truths impose, no needs can break their seal."

Ultimately, having abandoned common belief in metaphysical elsewheres, we have come to a place from whence we can proceed only in hope and hubris:

> We, the holders of Philosophy's new Bibles,
> look away from everything we know corrodes, and speak
>
> Pentecostally if cautiously of the Plan of Man, the engines
> of his mind's consistency, the freedom from delay his towers
>
> Know, forever rising from cartographies of hope!
>
> ('No Heaven Cold Enough')

The mutually-defining inseparability of life and death is engaged in numerous poems, most conspicuously in 'The Dead Have Plans', which is technically remarkable for its highly effective slant rhyme triplet form: "They fear the mirror they walk through is clouding, / There's nothing either side, and only colluding / Will keep the living and the dead from colliding". Porter moves among his own dead in a group of poems extending from memories of his parents and Brisbane childhood to wide views of Australia's past and present. 'Ranunculus Which My Father Called Poppy' movingly evokes his father's detachment in stoical loneliness through decades of widowhood lent meaning only by his love of gardening: "Our front gate is open, I watch him hobble-kneed / sifting his inch long plants from hessian – ranunculus / are hard to grow from seed."

'How the Eureka Stockade Led to Boggo Road Gaol' traces the rising fortunes of Porter's architect great-grandfather on the wave of Australia's growth from the mid-nineteenth century onward. The emphatic ballad rhythms and conversational directness of the poem gesture towards the Australian verse idioms of Lawson, Patterson, and other contemporaries of Porter's ancestor. The moral of the poem, however, commends the pioneer instinct to move away from origins that in turn set the course of Porter's own life:

> My Great-Grandfather, pioneer,
>   May help me to refuse
> To praise my country: he made clear
> Between New Start and Old Career
>   There isn't much to choose.

The voice we know as uniquely Porter's – the wry generosity, the declamatory boldness that is never strident, the gentleness untainted with sentimentality – is heard more clearly and directly than ever in this richly various collection. The last poem, 'River Quatrains', is a fitting finale in its stanzas' fluid movement through all their thematic turns:

> The River Jordan flows in semiquavers,
> The Seine runs on past Seurat's tingling dots,
> The dead on Ganges ghats burn next to bathers,
> The Acheron parts Haves from the Have-Nots.

The poem's close finds Porter looking into the future and beyond, confronting what he has achieved and, on the strength of this collection, has yet to achieve in its moment of visionary stocktaking:

> I'm on a river bank. I think I see
> The farther side: a choice of nothingness
> Or Paradise. My poems wait for me,
> They look away, they threaten and they bless.

Douglas Houston's *New and Selected Poems* is expected in 2010.

ℬ

THE GEOFFREY DEARMER PRIZE 2008

The annual Geoffrey Dearmer Prize is awarded to the best poem in the year's *Poetry Review* to have been written by a poet who has not yet published a full collection. We are extremely proud of this prize, which is in keeping with our enthusiasm for the very best of writing, regardless of reputation, and we are most grateful to the Dearmer family. Their generosity, which honours the noted WW1 poet and Society member, makes this celebration of emerging talent possible. In keeping with the tenor of this issue, the 2008 prize was judged by the thoroughly-emerged Peter Porter, one of our most distinguished poets.

Peter Porter

Considering poems by people who have not yet published a book is an excellent way of sampling how poets estimate stylistics at a particular time of crisis. I have chosen three from the nineteen poems published last year in *Poetry Review* which fit the Prize's requirements, all of which pay homage to already existing literary achievements. That the Present is so haunted by the Past seems a good thing to me.

Two of the poems are quite long and derivative in a highly personal way. Stephen Yeo's *Thank You Auden* is a witty, unfoggy and referential trawl through the mighty works of Uncle Wiz: Knowingness (and this is a very knowing poem) can be attractive, and no-one from any Dead Poets' Society is more fun to anatomise than Auden. Yeo acknowledges one of Auden's own household guides – the well-informed goddess, Gossip.

Paul Bentley's *Barnsley Abu, (A Postcard to Paul Muldoon)* is also very knowing, appealing as it does to a more recently celebrated writer. But Muldoon is only there by way of key signature – most of the poem is concerned with the social, political and, above all, footballing life of the North, a fine broth of lowbrow and highbrow people, names and enthusiasms.

The winning poem is Kearan Williams's *Chill*, an audacious modernising of Horace's *Ode I.XI*, the notorious 'carpe diem'. Notorious because it is a reef on which a whole fleet of translators have wrecked, usually spectacularly. As an all-too-fallible taker-up of Latin myself, I admire this version immoderately. Of course, it's anachronised, but is done with such lightness and skill as to be almost as good as Louis MacNeice's reworking of *Ode I.IV*, 'Solvitur acris hiems'. Abrupt, noisy and very jaunty. After all, Horace was not all decorum: he knew a lot about hard options:

Chill

After Horace, *Odes* 1.XI

Sweetheart, horoscopes never say: *Leo. Check the tyre pressure,*
or you'll plunge off the cliff road tomorrow. Cancer. It's got you.
Don't fight it. Goodbye. Let's just live our lives. If this is our last winter,
that's fine.
Down in the bay, the sea is endlessly crashed out on pebbles.

Come inside from the cold and the shore's ceaseless grinding.
Open another bottle. Let it breathe. Prune time hard back
to this moment. Hear me shushing you. Relax. It is now
and that matters. Be warm. Shut the window. Hold me. Here.

Kearan Williams

Kearan Williams was born in North Wales in 1960. She now lives near Cambridge, where she works as a librarian. In 1990 she attended poetry workshops run by Jo Shapcott. Up until then, she says, "I'd only *thought* about writing – those workshops made me do it. I had a few poems published in magazines, won 3rd Prize at Bridport in 1995, did a couple of Arvon courses, and read lots of contemporary poetry. Then family and work life got busier, and the poetry reading and writing slipped away. I started writing poems, and reading and thinking about poetry again, in 2006.

"Favourite poets I return to are: Gillian Allnutt, Paul Muldoon, Michael Hofmann, Jamie McKendrick, Don Paterson, Kathleen Jamie, Jo Shapcott, Elizabeth Bishop. The list could go on... I like poetry to be subtle, complex and resonant, with enough surface pleasure to lure and captivate the reader."

Williams's recent work has been published in *nthposition*, *Poetry Wales*, *Seam* and *Smiths Knoll*.

Lost Language

The last time we tried to talk:
a crackle in her voice like applewood
sparking. *I think she's trying to say something.*
Her eyes, when they lifted, incredibly
grey, as her speech powdered
down like falling snow.
                    Outside,
on the A-road, haulage and logistics.
Probably too late. Fading. Indistinct.
Now, at the end, intimate, withheld,
our lost conversations
heap and spoil at the graveside.

Funambule

My life so far, suddenly taut with it,
the chill bluster of history blowing through my clothes.
Stretched between the masted boats of my birth and death
are ropes, wires, and along them come
a troupe of women, their parasols dancing,
a ginger-hoofed horse with its cart of provisions,
wheel on wire, wire and wheel.
Listen! The tiny bells of hecklers;
the waft of carrion, rotting fruit,
the damp and mould flowering in my bones.
But there are fireworks, acrobats and supermarket trolleys.
My life is playing out as a sultan's şenlik,
and the air is filled with the twang of cold music.

CONTRIBUTORS

Tiffany Atkinson's first book was *Kink and Particle*. **Emily Berry** won an Eric Gregory Award in 2008. Her pamphlet collection, *Stingray Fevers*, is available from Tall-Lighthouse. **Alan Brownjohn**'s *Collected Poems* were published by Enitharmon in 2006. **Sasha Dugdale**'s translations include Elena Shvarts's *Birdsong on the Seabed* (Bloodaxe, 2008), and Chekhov's *Cherry Orchard* (BBC Radio 3, 2008). **Ian Duhig**'s *The Speed of Dark* (2007) was shortlisted for the T.S.Eliot prize. **Elaine Feinstein**'s new selection of translations of Marina Tsvetaeva is published by Carcanet in June 2009. **John Fuller**'s latest book is *Song and Dance* (2008). **David Grubb**'s *The Man Who Spoke to Owls* is due from Shearsman this May. **Martin Harrison**'s new book is *Wild Bees* (Shearsman, 2008). **Jane Holland** is the editor of *Horizon Review*; her latest poetry collection is *Camper Van Blues* (Salt). **Clive James**'s *Angels over Elsinore* is reviewed in this issue. **Alan Jenkins** received a Cholmondeley Award in 2006. **Judith Kazantzis** received a 2007 Cholmondeley Award. **Gwyneth Lewis** was the first National Poet of Wales. **Tim Liardet**'s *The Blood Choir* (2006) was shortlisted for the T.S.Eliot Prize. **Roddy Lumsden**'s fifth collection *Third Wish Wasted* is published by Bloodaxe in Spring 2009. He is currently preparing a major anthology, *Identity Parade: New British and Irish Poets*. **Andrew Motion**'s *The Cinder Path* is forthcoming from Faber. **Roger Moulson**'s first book *Waiting for the Night-Rowers* was a PBS recommendation, longlisted for The Guardian First Book Award and won the Jerwood Aldeburgh Prize. **Michael Murphy**'s latest publication is *Allotments* (2008). **Les Murray**'s *The Biplane Houses* was published in 2007. **Sean O'Brien** won the 2007 Forward and T.S.Eliot prizes with *The Drowned Book*. **Jeri Onitskansky** is a new poet. **Kathryn Simmonds**'s *Sunday at the Skin Launderette* (Seren) won the 2008 Forward Prize for best first collection. **Alan Stubbs** has been commended in the Arvon competition and shortlisted for the Bridport Prize. **George Szirtes**'s *New and Collected Poems* is just published by Bloodaxe. **Anthony Thwaite**'s *Collected Poems* was published in 2007 by Enitharmon. **Chris Wallace-Crabbe**'s *Telling a Hawk from a Handsaw* (2008) was a PBS Recommendation. **C. K. Williams**'s *Collected Poems* was published in 2006; he will publish a new book, *Wait*, in 2010. **Hugo Williams**'s *Dear Room* (2006) was shortlisted for the Costa Poetry Award.